MW00425552

LAO MIEN EMBROIDERY

Migration and Change

LAO MIEN EMBROIDERY

Migration and Change

Ann Yarwood Goldman

White Lotus
Bangkok Cheney

In loving memory of my son,

Martin Shin kyu Goldman

© Ann Yarwood Goldman, 1995. All rights reserved.

White Lotus Co., Ltd
G.P.O. Box 1141
Bangkok 10501
Thailand

Printed in Thailand

Typeset by COMSET Limited Partnership

ISBN 974-8496-41-4   pbk. White Lotus Co., Ltd.; Bangkok
ISBN 1-879155-54-0   pbk. White Lotus Co., Ltd.; Cheney

CONTENTS

PREFACE

Over the last two centuries groups of Iu Mien or Mien, a subgroup of the Yao, have migrated south from China into the mountains of northern Vietnam, Laos, Burma, and Thailand where they practice slash and burn agriculture growing rice, corn, and other crops. In these various isolated areas of Southeast Asia they have developed regional variations in clothing, customs, and language which distinguish them from each other and from the many other neighboring ethnic groups. They have also maintained their ties with China and have resisted change.

Mien men preserve their culture by recording their Taoist religious traditions in books written in Chinese, diligently teaching their sons to read and write this script and conduct ceremonies in this language, quite different from spoken Mien which until recently had no written form. Several of the ceremonial garments worn by male priests are distinctly Chinese in style and are still often purchased directly from China. Women strive to maintain harmony with the spirit world by keeping a proper Mien household and by teaching their daughters the embroidery designs and clothing traditions of their mothers and grandmothers.

During the Vietnam War in the 1960s, many thousands of Mien from northwestern Laos were forced to flee first from their villages and then from their country. They fled into Thailand where many stayed for years in refugee camps before being sent to a third country of resettlement such as France, Canada, or the United States. As of 1992, approximately 16,000 Mien had migrated to the United States, and at least 10,000 had settled in the state of California, with other significant populations in the states of Oregon and Washington. Almost all of these Mien came from the Lao province of Namtha, the rest essentially migrated from Sayabouri and Bokeo Provinces.

In 1978 when large numbers of Southeast Asian refugees were beginning to arrive in the San Francisco Bay Area, the International Institute of the East Bay signed me up as a volunteer in their refugee resettlement program. As an embroiderer and a weaver at the time, I was impressed by the wealth of hand-embroidered clothing which the Mien refugees wore, and I began to volunteer all my time with them. Going to airports, welfare offices and doctors' offices, I carried with me pieces of embroidery I was working on and got teased mercilessly because my needle was too big, my threads too short, and I embroidered on the incorrect side of the fabric.

In the days before there were any translators available, I quickly learned how challenging, enjoyable, and possible it was to communicate without a common language. I was as eager to learn about their customs as they were to learn about modern kitchens, schools, busses, and laundromats, as well as English, math, and filling out job applications.

In 1982 a group of Mien and American women including myself, founded the Laotian Handcraft Center in Berkeley, California in order to offer classes to previously uneducated Laotian refugee women and to provide a retail outlet for their needlework. Because of the large number of Laotian refugees in the area, the Center soon began to develop cultural programs for schools and to import articles and artifacts from Thailand and Laos for both American and Laotian customers.

As the years have gone by and the Mien have adjusted to life in the United States, only infrequently seeking outside help, my interest in their culture and in their adjustment to mine has grown. By the late 1980s I was making yearly trips to Thailand to scout for appropriate merchandise for the Laotian Handcraft Center store and to visit relatives of the Mien staff in villages in Northern Thailand. On two occasions I was able to extend my trips to Laos.

In 1991 the Laotian Handcraft Center received grants from the National Endowment for the Arts and the California Arts Council to do research on Mien embroidery. In 1991 and 1992 fifty interviews were conducted in Sacramento, San Jose, Oroville, Oakland, Richmond, and San Pablo, California by myself, by Sandra Cate, a graduate student in anthropology at the University of California at Berkeley, and by Muey Sio Fong, Mien coordinator and assistant store manager at Laotian Handcraft Center.

Most of the Mien women interviewed were born within a three days' walk of Namtha, capital of Namtha Province, Laos. A few were born in the Sayabouri and Bokeo Provinces of Laos, and one was born in China. Two were born before 1910 and nine between 1910 and 1935. Three were too young to have any memories of Laos. A few have converted to Christianity, but most still practice the traditional combination of Taoist and animist beliefs and practices.

The descriptions of embroidery in this book can be assumed to apply to embroidery from Namtha Province unless otherwise stated.

Every effort has been made to obtain information directly from the embroiderers themselves, all women. At four interviews husbands or sons generously helped with translation, but all other interviews were conducted in English or with the help of Meuy Sio Fong, herself a Mien embroiderer. Each person was interviewed in her own home, and frequently friends and relatives chose to participate informally, often adding valuable information.

For my trips to Thailand, Muey Sio Fong provided me with an introductory taped message to play in Mien villages explaining who I was, why I was interested in Mien clothing, and what I wanted to see. Other Mien salesclerks sent cassettes to their relatives announcing my arrival dates. I became a go-between, transporting gifts and cassette messages between relatives in Thailand and California. (1)

Interviewing Mien in California has been every bit as interesting and rewarding as visiting Mien villages in Thailand. The friendship, patience, cooperation, and hospitality shown by the many American Mien families we visited was invaluable and greatly appreciated.

Of special help were Muey Sio Fong, Meuy Yoon Phan, Muey Seng Chao, Ying Kwen Saeteun, Toud Kouei Law, and Liw Chian Saephan who recorded their life histories on tape and were also consulted continuously on specific topics such as the cost of clothes, the wedding ceremony, customs and changes pertaining to needlework, and learning to embroider. Muey Sio Fong and Fahm Ian Saelee provided invaluable help with the names and proper Mien spelling of the embroidery designs.

Other people who provided information and support were Elaine Lewis, author of *Peoples of the Golden Triangle*, Sylvia Lombard, and Lois Callaway, all missionaries who worked with the Mien and other hill people in Thailand over a period of many years and who were particularly interested in the women and their embroidery. Nancy Tingley at the San Francisco Asian Art Museum gave initial encouragement and editing help, and Jacqueline Butler-Diaz, author of *Yao Design in Northern Thailand*, arranged for viewing and photographing of the William Sage Collection of Lao Hilltribe clothing at the Arizona State University Museum of Anthropology. Dr. Herbert Purnel, David Cooke, Youd Sinh Chao, and Kao Man Sae Phan generously helped with the Mien word glossary. Karen Hipkins, Jane Hanks, Joel and Barbara Halpern, and Jack Kornfield all of whom lived, worked, or traveled in Laos either during the sixties or seventies lent photos, information, and embroidery they acquired during that time.

On my trips to Thailand Suwadee and Stephen Salmon assisted me tremendously with their insight, knowledge, and hospitality. In northern Thai villages, relatives of Mien in California were extremely gracious and helpful. And the staff of Ockenden Venture in Nan Province was very generous in providing transportation to mountain and lowland villages in that area. Professors Chetana and Tasanee Nagavajara and their daughters helped make Bangkok an interesting, hospitable, and navigable place. Linda D'Ari, my brother, Ed, and three of my children who accompanied me on various trips to Thailand offered physical help and much appreciated companionship and enthusiasm.

Thanks also go to Betsey Warrick and Barbara Voorhees-Emmons of the Laotian Handcraft Center who lent support for this project, and to my husband, George, who has been unfailingly patient and encouraging in my never-ending interest in all things Mien.

Photographs were taken by Sandra Cate (SC), Linda D'Ari (LD), Sylvia Lombard (SL), myself (AG), and one by Mey Meng Saeteun of her relatives in France.

INTRODUCTION

In less than twenty years, thousands of Mien have moved enormous physical and cultural distances, from the mountains of Southeast Asia to urbanized parts of the United States, from remote villages of fifteen to twenty families to the mazes of freeways and factories in a complex multi-cultural society. Here is Toud Kuei's experience of that move, describing her arrival in Salt Lake City, Utah, in 1983, to find her luggage gone:

"My clothes, my children's clothes, my husband's, my father's, my whole family's clothing, all the things we lost . . . lost five boxes. Then my little boy nine months old have clothing his grandparents give to him . . . I lost all my clothing, all my things made in Laos, old stuff. First I just sit there, I said I don't have anything . . . then I think in the United States I don't have to wear [Mien clothing] so that's O.K. But when I move here [Richmond, California] so many Laotian people they have Mien clothing I say O.K., I have to make new clothes. I buy some, I embroider some, so now I have the new."

Like Toud Kuei, each of the California Mien women interviewed told a unique story of that migration. Each has responded to the dramatic changes in her life with different strategies for survival and for redefining her personal and communal identity. Yet each also has reiterated the themes of Toud Kuei's narrative—trauma, loss, ambivalent attitudes towards embroidery, the need to have (but not to wear) Mien embroidered clothing. While still produced, with ever-increasing complexity and fineness of stitch, Mien clothing lies bundled in suitcases and baskets, in closets, and under beds.

In the highlands of southeast Asia, children began work at an early age—caring for younger siblings, tending cows, feeding pigs and chickens, gathering wild plants in the forest. Selected young Mien boys were taught to write, in Chinese, the ritual books which record Mien family and community history. In parallel fashion, young Mien girls were taught to embroider. Girls learned embroidery designs from their grandmothers, mothers, aunts, sisters and friends, thereby preserving Mien knowledge in patterns inspired by local plants, animals, household utensils, religious beliefs, and the designs of other hilltribes.

Many scholars have identified the key ethic in Mien culture as "wealth accumulation." The main goal of amassing wealth is to finance ceremonies which maintain beneficial relationships with ancestors and spirits—to ensure security and good fortune in this life and success in the afterworld. In Laos, the drive to accumulate wealth could be seen as a push for productivity in a number of cultural activities besides rituals: in multiple agricultural cycles, trade in opium, a high adoption rate to compensate for problems of infant mortality and infertility, the pressure on women to produce children, or brideprice.

For women, productivity is valued as "hard work," "good embroidery." When asked what qualities men looked for in Mien women, Muey Sio relpied that as young men went from village to village, "they just watch the hard worker, who can work on the farm, at home, can embroider good, is neat woman."

In addition to clearing land, tending fields, raising children, pigs and chickens, gathering firewood, pounding rice, cleaning houses, cooking for families and guests, making paper for ceremonial "spirit money," and dyeing cloth, Mien women embroidered and sewed clothing for the entire family, striving to produce a new set for each family member for the New Year's celebration.

Women's pants are particularly important. They carry many taboos, such as that related by one Mien woman: " . . . it's bad for a man to touch a woman's pants after they are worn . . . will make man sick." Women's pants set out to dry must not be hung higher than a man's head. When a woman marries and first goes to her husband's home to join his family, often the bride must walk under a pair of her mother-in-law's pants, as a gestural symbol of her future obedience and submission.

Given the enormous production time for embroidered clothing set against their duties in the fields and as hostesses for numerous large ceremonial gatherings, wealthy Mien women did not hesitate to pay or barter with others to embroider for them. Women often developed specialized skills—such as finger braiding the cord for jackets and baby carriers or cutting appliqué flowers—in exchange for food or supplies. According to Muey Sio, if women do not sew or are very poor, " . . . they have to wear the people's old clothes . . . Rich people make scarecrows out of old clothes, poor people don't have money to buy cloth and thread, they steal off scarecrows." Pet Fong told us that "some people have to work one, two days for old clothes . . . one day for old pants with holes, three or four days for something better."

So for Mien women, productivity translates in two directions. Productivity is fertility—bearing children who can help in the fields to increase the family's wealth, take care of their parents in their old age, and, most importantly, after their parents' deaths perform the merit-making ceremonies which insure and increase a person's status in the afterlife. A productive woman also sews at every spare moment—to create an abundance of clothing and a wealth of decoration on her pants.

During the Indochinese War, the Mien left their villages quickly with little preparation. Most took along all their clothing, but during the hardships of migration through the jungles—bombing, lack of food, fear, thieves, illness, and death—many sold their silver and ceremonial clothes for money and food. Major changes in embroidery designs and production began as Mien encountered Mien from other regions after their first evacuation to the Nam Thouei area of Laos, where they learned new designs and were able to spend much more time embroidering, as they were fed by U.S. military rice drops by parachute. There the Laotian Mien saw others embroidering the time-consuming cross-stitch on their pants. According to Muey Sio, "We thought, 'That's very nice, that's beautiful'."

Later in the refugee camps along the Thai-Lao border, where tribal peoples lived together, young Mien women began to wear Thai *phaa sin* (sarongs) because, said Nai Choy, "they were easier to wash, easier to make." Also women stopped wearing Mien clothing out of self-protection. In the camps, being recognizable as an ethnic minority could cause problems for them. As Liew Choy explained, if they wore "city clothes" . . . "the Thai not know what kind of people [we were]. They don't like Lao people."

By 1983, after Mien had begun settling in the United States, those remaining in the Thai camps began to produce traditional clothing, not for themselves, but for Mien in western countries. Informants have expressed the necessity of having the "new" clothing and of paying prices high enough to encourage increasingly finer, denser cross-stitch on all clothing pieces. An informal marketing network has developed within and between Mien communities internationally, based upon word-of-mouth information as to who is looking to buy, who has pieces to sell.

This network has had significant implications for Mien social life. Family relations largely based upon mutual assistance—a sharing and reciprocation of needlework skills across generations has been transformed into the exchange of goods for cash. Mothers no longer teach their daughters to sew. Women have taken on new roles outside the home, sometimes causing strains within their families. The competition of the market has stimulated aesthetic changes in the clothing itself: regional distinctions have disappeared. The Mien in Sacramento, California wear the same clothing as the Mien in Paris, France. For a time the Mien in the San Francisco Bay Area ordered a brilliantly-red yarn from relatives in France, to make the ruff for the jackets they had purchased from relatives in Thailand. Women are now buying a particular color of yellow embroidery floss to take to their relatives in China. Socio-economically, as well as symbolically, international communities of Mien are bound together by thread.

The market in Mien clothing has also intensified what I call the Mien "aesthetics of abundance"—the material expression of the Mien ethic of wealth accumulation. Everything on Mien clothing is "more": for example, more cross-stitch creates a much denser, more brightly-colored effect. Women use more yarn on the jacket ruff, and more rows of finger braid in more colors to anchor more applique flowers onto the baby-carriers worn as ceremonial capes. They apply more silver coins and finely-worked silver filigree decorations to the ceremonial baby-carriers.

Currently a single, complete woman's outfit costs several thousand dollars. Within local Mien communities the wedding costume consititutes the major portion of the bride price. The families of the bride and groom now negotiate the sharing of its costs, as well as that of the wedding celebration.

In the United States only a few older Mien women, who stay mostly at home, continue to wear Mien clothing every day. Whereas women's clothing was the key ethnic marker among hilltribes in the Southeast Asian highlands, in the refugee camps and in the United States where ethnic costume marginalizes those who wear it, Mien have conformed to the dominant culture.

Although they say they wear Mien clothing for New Year's parties, weddings, and other major ceremonies, Mien women rarely do so, except at two crucial times. The close female relatives of the bridal couple may wear "Mien" for major weddings; most guests do not. Mien women also wear traditional dress for their burial, layering three sets if they can afford them.

Weddings and funerals represent the two moments of connection for the Mien between this world and that of their ancestors and spirits. Mien weddings introduce the bride to the ancestors of her husband's family. Funerals, of course, expedite one's passage from this world to the next. Mien clothing in these two contexts reinforces the ties between themselves, their past ancestors, and their own future in the spirit world, affording them some sense of security and spiritual potency.

Having Mien clothing, but not wearing it, maintains essential relationships with the past and with the ancestral and spirit world, while enabling them to adapt to their current circumstances. It is significant also that Mien women still wear Mien clothing for photographs they send back to their families, suggesting that they still need to assert their identity within the larger Mien community of their past, represented by their relatives in Southeast Asia. Some have told us they wouldn't be recognized with short hair, in Western-style clothing. And to wear American clothing in photographs is considered boastful and inappropriate, while wearing expensive Mien clothing emphasizes their material successes in a culturally-approved manner. When they return to visit, however, Mien always wear American clothing, which gives them status in the Southeast Asian context.

When asked how they feel in Mien clothing, Mien women have answered, "hot." Young Jessica wore Mien clothing at her wedding. She complained, "The jewelry was heavy, the headpiece on my head. Just thinking of it gives me a headache . . . It's so heavy you forget about the hot part." That their first thought of Mien clothing is of its physical sensation—of being tightly bound with yards of cloth, feeling its weight, and its constrictions suggests the extent of Mien women's ambivalence towards it.

For Mien women these changes in the production and wearing of their clothing constitute, if not resistance to, a re-negotiation of their roles within the family and the community. In Laos, those who could afford to pay others to sew did. In the United States many more women, often holding two or three jobs, can now also afford to buy. They cannot be considered lazy since they have the clothing which expresses their wealth and their productivity. Thus purchasing clothing still upholds many Mien values without the onerous (for some) burden of having to make the clothing themselves. Many Mien women in the United States continue to embroider, because they enjoy it, because that "is what Mien women do," because they need to feel productive in a Mien way, but they no longer embroider because they must in order to have clothes to wear.

The increased "wealth" of Mien embroidered clothing on a bride or in a photograph simultaneously represents their intensified spiritual concerns and the improved material circumstances of their lives, as they become able to buy Mien clothing from other Mien. The significance of clothing for Mien women both as **Mien** and as **women** derives not only from its continuing display of wealth and productivity but also from its exchange within the social arena of family and international communities of Mien and within ongoing relations between themselves, their ancestors, and the spirits which rule their fate.

by Sandra Cate

SUPPLIES AND TECHNIQUES

SUPPLIES

The Lao Mien produce neither silk nor cotton, and they do not weave. Although one woman interviewed could remember a time in China when Mien women did weave, Laotian Mien long ago gave up their looms and now make garments from handspun, handwoven, even-weave cotton fabric purchased from neighboring peoples such as the Tai Leu, Tai Dam, Lantien, or Akha who grow, spin, and weave cotton.

Families purchase several bolts of this unbleached white cloth, *ndie-baeqc*, each year. New and undyed, it is used extensively in religious ceremonies. Long lengths are used in *guaax dang*, bridge, "catch the spirit", funeral, and other large ceremonies. (2) This cloth covers the table where a priest writes on paper money to be burned and sent to the spirit world. When a priest conducts a ceremony, he is given a bundle containing rice and coins wrapped up in this cloth. He is also given a strip of white cloth to wear around his waist during the ceremony. (3) Smaller pieces of white cloth are worn by certain individuals such as the children and siblings of the deceased at a funeral ceremony.

White cloth is also embroidered and used for the towels worn by the major participants in a wedding. (4) And a small piece of embroidered white cloth is sewn into the neck facing of every woman's coat. (5)

But for most clothing the bolts of fabric are first dyed several times in indigo, *njaamh*, and then over-dyed with other dyes from plants such as the vine, *nqimh diux*, to make them almost black. This dyed cloth is called *ndie-jieqv*, black cloth, or *ndie-maeng*, green cloth, referring to the color of the indigo dye bath. Muey Sio Fong recalls, "There are two kinds of indigo plants. One grows very easily and one is hard to grow, but it's better for dyeing." Muey Yoon Phan adds, "For indigo, we dye two weeks or longer once a day for one or two hours in a big tub covered with wood. Take out, drip, hang on bamboo racks to dry. Then put in again. We look to see if dye is good, when it all looks the same inside, outside. Then to make it really dark we have three kinds of plants. Some kind of ivy looks like blood inside. One kind we use the bark. It's big like a tree. We cook until all the color comes out very dark. After the indigo dyeing we put black sweet rice in to make the color stay. Next day put back into indigo again two or three times. Then we rinse and rinse until not too much color comes out. I helped my mother many, many times." (6)

Lao Mien purchase their embroidery threads, *fei* or *suix*, from neighboring tribes such as the Lahu and the Tai Dam or from Chinese traders who periodically come through the mountain villages. The thread is purchased undyed and then dyed with plant, insect, or powdered chemical dyes from China. Muey Yoon says, "Maroon, we have a plant which lowland people grow. They call *cuoh muoqc*. It's a little tree. We cut it and use the wood or roots. We also buy dye from lowland people or Chinese. Very expensive so we don't use too much."

Muey Sio says, "In our old village we used plants for the yellow color. We used the root of a plant that looks just like ginger. And the plant we call yellow steamed rice flowers, *hnaangx-zaang-yangh biangh*, is good for coloring rice (for the children) but not too good for thread. It doesn't stay too well. It's called butterfly bush here."

Before actually embroiderying, thread is almost always over-spun either on a drop spindle or by rolling it on the thigh to make it tight and strong. (8) Silk thread, being more expensive, is used sparingly, and since cotton and silk take the dye color differently, silk tends to be used for certain colors like dark maroon. Commercial thread was generally not available to the Namtha Mien until they began to move south toward Thailand in the 1960s, therefore the presence of pearl cotton on a pair of pants can sometimes help date it.

Thread has significance for the Mien in areas other than needlework. Thread can connect or transmit between this world and the spirit world. Thread can tie a person's soul, or well-being, inside the body. Scissors, on the other hand, can cut away the bad influences. Threads and scissors are used in many Mien religious observances. (3, 7)

Supplies for embroidery are kept in an open sewing basket, *ndaan*. This is generally made of woven bamboo and rattan and stands on short legs. It contains needles, *sim*, scissors, *njiuv*, spools and skeins of thread, some in pre-measured overspun bundles ready for embroidery, packets of dye brought or sent from Laos or Thailand, drop spindles, glasses, beads, small pieces of fabric, sample cloths, braided cording, silver buttons, silver wire, the embroidery wrapper, and work in progress. It also serves as a storage container for innumerable odds and ends such as bottles of pills, shoelaces, small change, keys, nail clippers, and so on. (9, 64)

EMBROIDERING, *CONGX CONGX*

Mien women spend much time embroidering and sewing the distinctive garments that identify both men and women visually as Mien. (12) But the four most frequently used garments, worn by a Mien woman in Laos day and night throughout the year, are the fully embroidered pants, turban, sash, and long coat. The pants, having by far the most embroidery on them, take the most time to make and are the most visible daily expression of a woman's needle skills. They most clearly record the changes that have occured in Lao Mien embroidery.

Traditionally, no matter what the woman's circumstances, the embroidered pants were a necessity. If a woman was very poor she could work for a family who would give her old pants as payment. If a family needed all the women for farm work someone else could be hired to make the pants, but it was unthinkable not to have them.

In Mien villages it is still inconceivable for a girl not to learn to embroider. The women say, "If we don't learn how to embroider, we will have no clothes to wear." It is an essential part of being Mien. Young girls eagerly await the day when they are first given a pair of embroidered pants to wear by their mother or an aunt. Muey Seng remembers, "We saw the people wear and we like it, and we tell parents we want pants, and they make one. About five or six years old. Later on we have to do, too. We have to study. Maybe eight years old we make our own." All girls strive from an early age to master the embroidery techniques so they will "not have to wear plain pants like a man." A young girl can sew pieces of embroidery for others, such as the leg gusset piece, in exchange for embroidery thread or a piece of fabric. She might also give a gift of embroidery to someone who has taught her, in this way convincing her mother that she has acquired the skill necessary to begin her own pair of pants.

Embroidery is the skill and activity that most clearly defines a good Mien woman, much as the ability to read and write Chinese defines a refined Mien man. On the three days of New Year, when Mien strive to set a pattern of good behavior for the coming year and when everyone is exempted from outside chores, mothers are expected to teach their daughters to embroider while the fathers teach the sons to write Chinese.

During the Vietnamese war, one of the American pilots involved in operations in Laos observed that Mien women spent all their time embroidering clothing. He suggested sending photos and samples of the embroidered pants to Hong Kong to have them reproduced commercially giving the Mien women more spare time. But the Mien leaders said that embroidery was traditional and they didn't want the women to give it up.

According to Lois Callaway, there was a time in the 1970s when Chinese traders tried to sell fabric, printed to look just like embroidered Mien pants' panels, to Mien villagers in the mountains of Northern Thailand. No one bought it.

1. *Mien in a northern Thai village holding photos, just received, of American Mien relatives. Note indigo-dyed hands. 1988. AG*

2. *Bridge ceremony in Richmond, California. 1990. Bridge is covered with a bolt of white cloth. Threads surround the bridge on the poles and connect it to the main bedroom in the house. AG*

3. *Priest conducting a bridge ceremony wearing tunic, hair hat, and white sash. San Pablo, California, 1994. AG*

4. *Wedding towel. Family heirloom owned by Ley Seng Saephan, Oakland, California. SC*

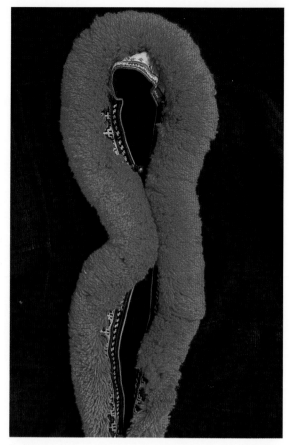

5. *Woman's coat. Red wool ruff and embroidered front and neck facings with white patch. Made by Mey Charn Saephan, 1978, in a Thai refugee camp. Ann Goldman collection. AG*

6. *Indigo-dyed bolts of cloth drying in a Thai Mien village. 1988. AG*

7. *Scissors and wood knife to cut away bad spirits and thread to keep good spirits close at a ceremony in Richmond, California. 1991. AG*

8. Cheng Xiang Saechao over-spinning thread on a drop spindle. Oakland, California. 1991. SC

9. Woman embroidering in Oroville, California. 1991. SC

10. Liw Chian Saechao embroidering. Richmond, California. 1994. AG

11. Finished pants' panel, left, and one in progress, right. Finished rows are wrapped to keep clean. Note yellow counting thread and outline stitches in unfinished area. Liw Chian Saechao. Richmond, California. 1994. AG

12. Mien men and women from Moung Sing, Laos, in traditional clothing. Nam Kueng, Laos, in the 1960s. SL

13. Close-up of stitches on a pants' panel showing rows of weave-stitch, stem-stitch, grid-stitch, and at the top, cross-stitch. Made by Koy Choy Saelee in 1978 in Chiang Kham Refugee Camp, Thailand. Front side on left, reverse side on right. Ann Goldman collection. AG

14. Detail of wedding towel showing braiding and chain-stitch border. Made by Kae Tso Saeyang's great-grand-mother before 1900. It was carried with other clothes in baskets on pack horses when fleeing northern Laos. The family had to go along stream beds and the baskets got wet, but they couldn't stop to dry things for three days so the colors ran. It appears to have Chinese characters embroidered on it. Signed? If so, it is unusual. Ann Goldman collection. AG

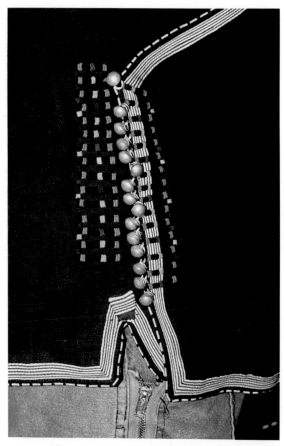

15. Man's jacket detail showing silver buttons, braid buttonholes secured with decorative buttonhole stitch, and edging braid wrapped with silver wire. Borders are narrow bands of appliquéd fabric. Jacket offered for sale by Mien refugees in Chiang Kham Refugee Camp, Thailand. 1990. LD

16. Man braiding with bobbins on a frame in Chiang Kham Refugee Camp, Thailand. 1990. LD

18. Appliquéd and embroidered baby carrier made by Liw Chian Saechao in 1982 for her daughter-in-law to wear at her wedding. Later all the silver was removed and it was, and is, used to carry babies. Now it is quite worn and has had several "spirits" tied onto it from ceremonies for the well- being of various children. Richmond, California. AG

17. Baby carrier. Plain, sparcely decorated carrier for daily use from northern Thailand. Ann Goldman collection. AG

19. Detail of ceremonial baby carrier with silver ornaments attached. On newer baby carriers such as this the appliqued pieces are edged with blue, not white flat braid. Liw Chian Saechao. Richmond, California. AG

20. Heirloom pants made in Laos or China over 50 years ago. Owned by Muey Seng Chao's family, Richmond, California. SC

21. Bottom weave sections of three pairs of pants made by Fahm Kouei Saelee, Oakland, California. Each pair is embroidered with a different weave- stitch design which reflect where she was living when she made it. AG

22. *Central or spider sections on three pairs of pants. The pair on the left was made in Chiang Kham Refugee Camp, Thailand, by Nai Chioe Saechao in 1979, the central pair is the old style from northern Laos, and the one on the right shows the red color of Chiangrai Province, Thailand. All are now out of style. Ann Goldman collection. AG*

23. *Different versions of the jung hungh or dragon design (across bottom third of photo). Left and center made by Tsan On Saelee, 1970, in Huei Orh, Laos, right by Chio Kuang Saechao, 1976, Nan Province, Thailand. Ann Goldman collection. AG*

24. *Different versions of Chinese Stairs or Thai Houses design in the large section near top left and in the fourth row down, second from left. Ann Goldman collection. Parts of this design can be found in several rows of the new pants, right, which have fragmented versions of many older designs. From Thailand, 1993. Muey Sio Fong, Richmond, California. AG*

25. *Different borders on the tops of Mien women's pants. From left: da'jungh Tree, Silver Flower, Little Girl Embroidery, Many Hands and Feet or Water Bug, Spaced Gibbon, Chinese Characters, Spider. Ann Goldman Collection. AG*

26. Old woman, Nan Province, Thailand, wearing new pants for New Year made with stylish colors but using old, widely spaced weave- and grid-stitch designs on coarsely woven fabric. Note red under-turban. AG

27. Northern Thai Mien women plucking forehead hairs by running twisted thread across skin. 1950s. SL

28. Young female relatives of the bride arranging their finery at a wedding in San Pablo, California. 1994. The back ornaments are attached under the coat ruff. AG

29. Ceremonial baby carriers covered with silver decorations and elaborate silver chains, tassels, pendants, and bells adorn women at a Mien wedding. The tops of the silver back ornaments (28) can be seen under the baby carriers. San Pablo. 1994. AG

30. Turban made by Yien Sio Saechao in Chiang Kham Refugee Camp, Thailand, in 1978. One end shows old-style designs and colors, other end is done in solid cross-stitch designs. The central embroidery is unusually intricate and colorful for a turban. SC

31. Liw Chian Saechao and her daughter, Muey Sio Fong. Liw Chian wears the old style turban, and Muey Sio wears a newer turban with bright blue embroidery and a central embroidery section. Richmond, California. 1994. AG

32. Comparison of old and new sash and turban ends. Cross-stitching appears on borders and blue replaces white threads on newer garments. Ann Goldman collection. AG

33. Mien children, northern Thailand, 1950s. Except for the baby hats, they are wearing smaller versions of the same garments worn by adults. The girls' pants, with a minimum of embroidery, were probably made for them by a mother or aunt. SL

34. Baby hats. Girl's hat, left, made by Koy Saechao in Laos, 1977. Boy's hat, right, made by Liew Choy Saechao in Chiang Khong Refugee Camp in 1980. Ann Goldman collection. AG

35. *Detail of boy's hat (34) showing appliquéd designs edged with flat white braid, silver decorations, band of cross-stitching, and round braid wrapped with silver wire on bottom edge. Ann Goldman collection. AG*

36. Boy's jacket made in Sacramento, California, by Liew Choy Saechao for her son. Braided edging is embellished with decorative buttonhole stitch. Ann Goldman collection. AG

37. Man's sash, old northern Laos style. Rows of chain stitch and braid on the border. Made in 1966 by Maun Choy Saephan in Nam Thouei, Laos, for her husband after their house and all their clothes had burned. Ann Goldman collection. AG

38. Man's silk vest that belonged to Muey Seng Chao's father-in-law in Laos. The buttons are old silver coins. SC

39. Mien religious painting showing Faam-Cing, the three gods who guard the highest level of the heavens. A bird named for these three important dieties is represented in the embroidery design, Faam-Cing Nqun, the Comb of the Faam-Cing bird. Ann Goldman collection. AG

40. Mien religious painting showing young male initiate in woman's coat climbing a sword ladder in an ordination ceremony. Ann Goldman collection. AG

41. Parents and relatives wrap red turbans and arrange wedding towels and jewelry on the groom and his attendants at a wedding in San Pablo, California. 1992. AG

42. Man's religious garments worn on the head while conducting religious ceremonies. Family heirlooms of Moang Kuei Saechao, San Jose, California Made in China in the 1920s. SC

43. Man's religious garments and sash in new colors. Fuei Chien Saelee, Richmond, California. SC

There are restrictions and taboos regarding embroidery. When an older family member dies, men aren't allowed to write, and women can't use a needle until the funeral is finished. Likewise, when a baby is born, the mother shouldn't embroider for several days or up to a month if she is unwell. Because thread is used in many ceremonies to symbolically connect the real world to the spirit world, it is believed that during a woman's pregnancy, her sewing basket should not be stored in her bedroom, and she should not embroider there. By defying this taboo the unborn baby, who is sent from the spirit world, might get stitched to the womb and have a difficult time being born. Similarly, during the infrequently conducted but very important *zoux ndaangh* ceremony, women must not embroider for fear they will stitch the angry spirits to the family.

DESIGN NAMES

Although design names often make reference to important aspects of their religion and the everyday world, the women interviewed consistently told us that they picked designs because of their beauty or because everyone else used them, not because they had any special significance. Often they did not know the names of designs they used, and there was frequent disagreement over some names since women from different villages attach different names to the same design. Some women gave derogatory names like "pig pooh" to designs they felt were hopelessly out of style and therefore ugly. When the name of the design seemed to refer to something from Mien religion, the women could rarely explain it fully. For instance, none of the women could satisfactorily explain the name of one of the oldest weave stitch designs, *Wuonh Guangv*, even though they had all heard it used in ceremonial songs and in traditional stories. Some said it was a kind of spirit, some said it was a man's name, and some said it was simply the name of the design, nothing else. They apologized and told us we would have to ask the men since only men can read the religious books and fully understand the religion. But, for the most part we decided to take our knowledge of the embroidery from the embroiderers themselves and not to ask the husbands or religious leaders for meanings of which the women were unsure.

The names Mien women choose to give to their designs contain a great deal of cultural information and often evoke fond memories of life in Laos. A few seeds of popcorn, *ga'maeqc mbeux*, were planted each year, and dry kernels were thrown into the fire for the benefit of the children who watched them pop and then retrieved them with chopsticks. A small black bird, *mba'hinx*, often built its nest in the house thatch and would "talk" to the household. Some women claim this bird brings good luck. When building a house or an irrigation system, poles are used to support, *caengx*, the cross pieces. In *congx-caengx* the central part of the design supports the rest of the embroidery.

ga'maeqc mbeux
popcorn

congx-caengx
supporting embroidery

mba'hinx dueiv
mba'hinx tail

3

Many designs are a reminder of the importance of plants and agriculture in the lives of the Mien. *Fam,* to fill spaces between embroidery designs, also means to reseed spaces where rice or other plant seeds fail to germinate. *Buih dorh* refers to the weights of balance scales which are used to weigh produce and seeds, and *jouv coix biangh* is the flower of the Chinese leek plant.

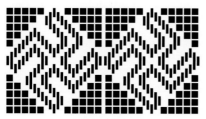

jienv with *fam* design
gibbon with filler design

buih dorh
scale weight

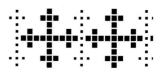

jouv coix biangh
Chinese leek flower

The Mien name or names of the designs have been written in italics, and translations are given to the extent possible. Even though a standardized Mien script has been in use since 1984, spelling can pose problems because very few Mien have learned to write their own language, and there are as yet no standardized dictionaries. The younger people are the most likely to have learned the script, but in the United States the Mien verbal skills of the young people are rapidly dwindling, and many have a much smaller Mien vocabulary than their parents. Mien is a tonal language, and many young people have difficulty recognizing tones. Fahm Ian Saelee, who was the initial spelling consultant for this book, is in her twenties and often did not know the design names. Muey Sio Fong, in her late thirties, gave her the names with the proper tonal pronunciation so that she could attempt to spell them correctly. For clues on how to pronounce the Mien words, refer to the Mien word glossary.

STITCHES

There are several stitches used by the Mien for their embroidery, but only three are used for the majority of the needlework: the weave-stitch, the grid-stitch, and the cross-stitch. (13) The oldest of these is probably the weave-stitch, *congx-jiemc,* which used to be the only stitch used on the women's pants. Looking very much like designs still handloomed by the Yao in China, it is considered the hardest to learn, but once the stitch sequences are memorized, it is considered the fastest embroidery technique.

Specific weave-stitch designs are always done on the bottom section of the pants. The stitches are done over and under either one, three, or five background threads in a set sequence according to the desired design. On the bottom section of the pants, the weave-stitch is done parallel to the warp threads of the background material, but on the upper body of the pants it is worked parallel to either the warp or weft threads. Separate design motifs are usually done in one single color, but for the continuous bands of weave-stitch at the bottom of the pants, pre-measured maroon, black, and white threads create adjacent sections. On modern pants additional colors have been added. In this book, diagrams indicating weave-stitch designs are done with short parallel lines.

Ga'maeqc mbeux
Popcorn. Weave-stitch

The grid-stitch, much like the Holbein-stitch, is called *congx-tiu, tiu* meaning to pick up. This stitch, like the weave-stitch, is worked parallel to the warp and weft of the background fabric, usually over and under two threads at a time forming a lacy-looking grid work of tiny boxes. Each grid-stitch design is worked in only one color, with white traditionally being the predominant color used. Bright blue has now almost completely replaced the white, but most women continue to call this new blue color *fei-baeqc* or white thread. Grid-stitch designs, like weave-stitch designs, are executed by embroidering a set sequence of stitches which young girls are expected to memorize.

som zaqc
straight *som*. Grid-stitch.

The cross-stitch, *congx-nyiet*, which means to tie up, used to be used on only a limited number of small or ceremonial items and never on women's pants. It is now rapidly replacing both the grid- and weave-stitches. On the reverse side of the fabric, the side on which the work is done, this stitch appears like the grid-stitch, but on the front it forms diagonal crosses covering two background threads in each direction. These crosses are depicted as squares in the diagrams. Some of the older cross-stitch designs are done with single rows of cross-stitching in one color such as the *m'zuv huaa* design. In these cases the background fabric provides the contrasting color. (4, 42)

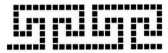

M'zuv huaa
M'zuv flower. Cross-stitch.

On modern clothing, most areas of cross-stitching completely cover the background fabric, therefore the designs are only distinguishable by a change of thread color. Thus, it requires the use of large amounts of thread and encourages the use of many colors. In the diagrams of cross-stitch designs, it can usually be assumed that the spaces without squares are also filled in with cross-stitching of contrasting colors. (89, 95) Unlike the weave- and grid-stitches, the cross-stitch designs do not need to be learned by an arduous memorization of stitch sequences. A girl does not have to learn them from her mother, who might not have much patience with a slow learner. She needs only an outline of a desired pattern, and from there she is free to employ her own creativity, within the bounds of a rather rigid Mien conformity, in completing the design.

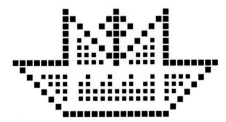

faam-cing nqun
Comb of the *faam-cing* bird. Cross-stitch.

The only other stitch used to any extent on women's pants is the stem-stitch, *njiuc*. It is used for the straight lines between different rows of embroidery. It is generally the first stitch Mien girls learn. This stitch is worked over four threads horizontally and one thread vertically. Each stitch overlaps the last one by two threads thus forming a solid line of slightly diagonal stitches. Rows of stem-stitch are usually done in groups of three, and as with the other stitches, color trends are changing. Fahm Ian says, "Now they change. If they want any color, they just put it, but the old people always used yellow, then red, then white."

Other stitches used are *binh zangv*, for hemming, *ziem*, which is a variation of the chain-stitch and is used for decorative edgings, (14), and *gaeng*, which is like a button hole stitch and is used to bind the top of tassels, to fasten braiding onto fabric and as a netting to cover decorative beads, coins, or good luck amulets. (15)

Except for the chain-stitch and one or two very old weave-stitch designs such as *mbiauz-mbungv*, fish bones, done on leggings, (57, 58) all embroidery is worked on the reverse side of the fabric, and the finished piece should be as tidy on the back as on the front. (13) Thread ends and any long lengths of thread between designs are carefully worked into the previous stitches. Mien embroiderers tend to use very long lengths of thread and to premeasure what they will need for one design. Older women often splice the ends of their thread.

BRAIDING

Braided cording, *hlaang*, is used as edging on many garments and accessories. For short lengths it is woven on the fingers, *gitv hlaang*, with loops of cotton or silk thread. Longer lengths are done with bobbins, *ndioux hlaang*, on a frame. The bobbin braiding is often done by men. (16) There are several braid variations. In its flat form, it is used to edge and attach appliqued designs to a background fabric, (18, 35), and as a round braid, sometimes wrapped at regular intervals with silver wire, it is sewn to the edge of cuffs, neck facings, sash ends and the like. (14, 15) Red or maroon and white are the traditional colors used as edging braid on most garments and white, green, and yellow for applique work, but on modern appliqué work blue flat braid has generally replaced white. (19)

APPLIQUE

Applique designs or flowers, *biangh*, which are cut from red or black cotton fabric, are often cut and applied by specialists who preserve paper patterns. They take the forms of butterflies, sunflowers, crabs, and other motifs from nature and are sewn to baby carriers and hats, kneeling blankets, and shoulder bags. (18, 35, 52, 62) Muey Sio remembers that in Laos her uncle knew how to cut the applique pieces. He lives in California now and doesn't do it anymore. She says that many people, who had spare time in the refugee camps, learned to cut fancy applique pieces, not like the simple ones people used in the past. Many people in the United States do it now, but she doesn't know of any men. The applique designs are edged with flat braiding.

Also appliqued are the very narrow strips of fabric sewn as borders on jacket and coat sleeves, *lui-leiz*, baby carriers, and blankets. (8, 15, 18)

CLOTHING AND ACCESSORIES

EVERYDAY GARMENTS FOR WOMEN

Women's pants, *sieqv dorn houx*

Mien women's pants consist of two rectangular embroidered leg panels joined to a large, loose, crotch section, smaller embroidered leg gusset pieces, *houx-caamv*, and a wide waist band. (20) The two rectangular panels which become the embroidered part of the pants are divided into horizontal sections marked off with rows of stem-stitch. Starting at the bottom there are three weave-stitch rows which alternate with two rows of the *som* design done in grid-stitch. The bottom row of weave-stitch is called *congx-dorn* or small embroidery, the middle one is *domh congx*, large embroidery, and the top one is *congx-setv*, edging or finishing embroidery.

som
Blocked or covered by a fallen tree

There are three distinct variations in the weave patterns done on this bottom part of the pants, and the one used depends on where and when the pants were made. (21) The one considered the oldest has several names. The women from Namtha Province call it *congx-nzaangc*, Chinese characters, or *congx-mbiaapc* refering to a fan used in religious rituals by priests. The *congx-nzaangh* design is still used by Mien in other parts of Laos and in Thailand where it is called *congx-ceix* or spike embroidery. (80, 82)

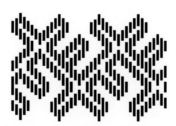

Congx-nzaangh, (congx-mbiaapc, congx-ceix)
Chinese characters (fan, spike)

But in Namtha Province about fifty to sixty years ago *congx-nzaangh* design was replaced by another variation,*Wuonh Guangv congx*. Since about 1960 the *Wuonh Guangv* design has in turn been completely replaced by *sopc biangh* or pumpkin blossom, the pumpkin or squash figuring prominently in one of the origin stories of the Mien. This design is considered by the

Namtha Mien to be much more beautiful and difficult than the previous variations, and although its use on women's pants is relatively recent, an almost identical design can be found on women's white ceremonial sashes that are over a hundred years old. (58)

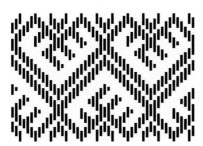

Wuonh Guangv congx
Wuonh Guangv embroidery

sopc biangh
pumpkin blossom

Except for these three variations the designs on these bottom five rows of embroidery have remained relatively unchanged over the years. However, the colors have undergone considerable change, with bright blue, green, red, and even yellow now seen where only maroon, black, and white were seen twenty years ago.

This bottom section, *houx-zaux*, pant leg, is usually followed by a row of spaced gibbon or *jienv* designs done in either weave- or grid-stitch. (20, 82, 90) Gibbons are often seen and hunted in the mountains of Laos, and as one woman explained, they produce a wax like bees' wax in their arm pits which is very hard to get because it falls off when the animal comes down to the ground. It is very powerful and can bring good fortune to those who have it. And if a little bit is rubbed on the clothing of a person of the opposite sex, it will make that person fall in love with you.

Jienv-jiemc
Gibbon, weave stitch

Jienv -tiu
Gibbon, grid stitch

Above the row of gibbons is the *houx-sin*, the body of the pants. On older pants there is a section bordered on both sides by a row of *som* designs, in white on Namtha pants and in alternating colors on pants of Thai or Sayabouri Mien. Between these borders is a row of the *lomh zeuv* designs. (20)

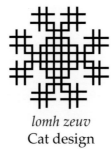

lomh zeuv
Cat design

8

Above this narrow section is a wider section called the spider embroidery, *congx-ga'nyorc,* containing groups of embroidery designs, such as the spider, *lomh zeuv,* baby pig's hoof, and popcorn. These designs are embroidered in grid- or weave-stitch with white, maroon, green, and yellow threads. Parts of this section are sometimes done with dark blue or black thread making them almost invisible on the dark background fabric. Groupings in the spider section with black design elements are called black spiders, *ga'nyorc-jieqv.* (20, 22, 90)

dungz-dorn deih
baby pig's hoof, weave-stitch

ga'nyorc
spider, grid-stitch

maeqc mbeux
popcorn, weave-stitch

On the more recently made pants both of these sections, traditionally filled with spaced designs set off by the dark color of the background fabric, have been replaced by numerous narrow rows of solid, elaborate, and colorful cross-stitch designs. Although the spider design and other grid- and weave-stitch designs are now rarely used on this part of the pants, Western Mien from Namtha Province still refer to this section as the spider section. (11, 103)

The spider is an appropriate motif as the Mien view spiders as having many of the attributes desirable in a woman. They are beautiful, industrious and dexterous. Women are often compared to spiders in song. Historically, it was a spider's web that guided a lost boat full of migrating Mien to shore, and symbolically the spider is one form taken by the spirit that guards an individual's well-being.

Cross-stitch designs with names reflecting the physical and spiritual world of the Mien such as tiger claws, big blossom, rice steamer, rainbow, and dragon now fill this upper part of the pants. Some reflect the contact the Mien have had with other groups of people: Chinese, or Thai, houses, Hmong umbrella, Hmong flower. (24, 97)

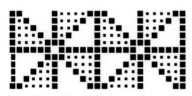

jung-hungh, jung-hinc
dragon, rainbow

domh biangh dueiv
big blossom tail

janx-gekv tei, janx-taiv biauv
Chinese stairs, Thai houses

nda'maauh nyiuv
tiger's claws

9

Each of the many designs has several variations. (23, 24)

Three variations of *jung-hungh*, dragon, design.

At the top of the pants panel, the embroiderer usually puts a final row of *som* done in grid-stitch or *congx-sieqv* in weave-stitch. Or she adds a final row of more widely spaced weave-stitch designs such as *wuom-gaeng*, water bug, or *jienv-saa*, a variation of the gibbon design.

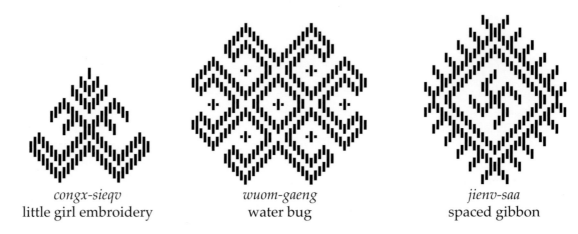

| *congx-sieqv* | *wuom-gaeng* | *jienv-saa* |
| little girl embroidery | water bug | spaced gibbon |

The water bug appears in a Mien story as the daughter of the powerful *jung-hungh*, or water dragon. The dragon is grateful to a fisherman for removing a fish hook from his mouth so he gives him his daughter, the water bug, who can take the human form of a beautiful woman and eventually brings wealth to the poor fisherman.

Other designs occasionally appearing at the top of women's pants are various forms of *nyaanh biangh* or silver flower, resembling the silver ornaments given to brides and grooms and *mba'ong don*, thunder stool. Thunder is a powerful force for driving away evil spirits. (25)

nyaanh biangh
silver flower

mba'ong don
thunder stool

The amount of embroidery on the pants' panels depends on the height, age, and work load of the person doing the embroidery. A short person will need less embroidery than a tall person. A girl making her first pair of pants might make only a few rows using the designs she has learned. A poor or older person or one with no time to embroider might put only a few of the bottom rows on her pants with some widely spaced designs above done in the more economical weave- or grid-stitch. (26, 86) But the ideal is a pair of pants with leg panels fully embroidered from the lower calf almost to the waist. The bottom edge of the pants is hemmed and trimmed with white and maroon braiding.

Woman's coat, *sieqv dorn lui*

To cover the upper part of her body, a Mien woman makes a long, ankle-length black coat that opens down the front and has waist-high openings in the side seams enabling her to bring up the front panels of the coat and tuck them into her sash allowing her embroidered pants to show.

The neck edge and front opening above the waist are covered with an embroidered facing, white at the back of the neck, *lui-jaang-nqom,* and black in the front, *lui-laeng.* (5) For young girls this embroidery is usually a simple weave-stitch pattern called *ga'maeqc mbeux,* popcorn, done in white thread. Brides and older women use an old cross-stitch pattern called *Luh Guon-louc* which is also used on articles of ritual significance like the bride's wedding hat square and the priest's tasseled band. (44, 56)

maeqc mbeuxx
popcorn

Luh Guon-louc
trailing *Luh Guon* design

The embroidered facing is then covered with a red wool ruff, *lui-guaan,* which was traditionally made from silk tassels placed at intervals along the neck edge, but is today made from twelve to fifteen balls of red yarn cut in short lengths, stitched very closely together and trimmed to form one long, smooth, thick, highly visible red border on the woman's coat, completely hiding the embroidery underneath. Liw Chian says, "My grandmother used a cotton ruff. You could see the embroidery on the neck edge. When I was fifteen years old the yarn came. Very expensive. I bought it one time. When you see it, it is very beautiful and you want it. The Chinese brought it from a long way on a horse. Long ago they used cotton string and dyed it red. I used to use this kind. Rich people used silk."

The sleeve cuffs are trimmed with narrow appliqued strips of red, black, and white cotton fabric, *liu-leiz.* Modern coats, however, often display blue strips of applique. This trim and the side openings are often edged with a border of braiding sometimes wrapped at regular intervals with silver wire, *finx.* The top of the side slit is further decorated with beads, *zou,* and long tassels, *nyueic,* made of red cotton, wool, or silk thread. (106)

The front opening is closed with a simple round silver button and looped button hole, but for special occasions, a woman displays a series of eight to ten large, flat, rectangular silver buckles, *la'kaux-mbeih,* down the front of her coat.

Woman's turban, *m'nqorngv-beu,* and sash, *la'sin*

The sash and the turban are quite similarly made, both comprising approximately six yards of black indigo-dyed cotton fabric embroidered on the ends. The sash which is worn wrapped around the waist over the coat tends to have wider bands of embroidery on the ends, and when tied, these colorful ends hang down the back of the coat. (74)

The turban, in addition to the embroidered ends, usually has embroidery placed along the center that shows when wrapped diagonally around a woman's head. This central embroidery, *danh jauv congx,* or middle-of-the-road embroidery, is a fairly recent addition, and many women from northern Laos had never seen it before they left their mountain villages in the early 1960s. (30, 31, 112) Mien women are expected to wear their turbans day and night. They are not supposed to expose their hair. Traditionally, a smooth, high forehead was admired, so women plucked out hair along the forehead and temples. "Weeds are growing in your rice field" might jokingly be said to a woman whose hair was showing. (27)

The embroidery designs on these two garments has not changed very much over the years, and the *som* and *lomh zeuv* patterns continue to be the standard ones used. But the colors have changed as they have on all the other embroidered garments with all the white being replaced by bright blue and with many other bright colors added as well. It is also considered fashionable now to substitute a row of cross-stitching for the row of *som* at the ends of the sash. (32) Both sash and turban are now often edged with silver-wrapped braiding.

lomh zeuv

som

Women like to wear an additional plain turban underneath the embroidered one, both for hygiene and to give a bigger, fuller shape. Some Thai Mien women use a red under-turban which shows on the top of their heads in the center of their turbans. (26, 102)

Baby carrier, *suangx-buix*

Another garment used frequently is the baby carrier which can be decorated quite simply, for its practical purpose of carrying a baby on the back (17), or can be elaborately decorated for ceremonial use. It is made from a large rectangle of indigo cloth, pleated at intervals along the top edge, which is sewn to a band forming the top border of the garment. This band is frequently appliquéd with strips of red and white or green cotton fabric over-stitched with yellow thread. At each end of this band long sashes are attached for securely wrapping the baby in the carrier onto a person's back. The ends of the sashes are decorated with colored bands, braiding, and beaded tassels. (18) The main body of the baby carrier is embellished with appliqué, embroidery, and, on the ceremonial garment, with many pounds of silver ornaments. (29)

The embroidery is done in grid- and cross-stitch. Tiger designs in cross-stitch, only recently appearing on Mien pants, have long been used on the baby carrier and other ceremonial garments and accessories. The tiger is considered the king of all animals, strong and protective, and appears in the ceremonial paintings used in Mien religious rituals. But when asked about the significance of tiger designs, one woman simply said, " We see tiger tracks and then copy them. Lots of tigers in Laos. Tiger skin designs are beautiful."

nda'maauh biorngh, nda'maauh m'normh
tiger forehead, tiger ears

Pieces of red fabric cut in the form of flowers, butterflies, and other nature motifs are appliqued onto the main body of the baby carrier. These designs are edged with flat white braid and often embellished with two-color yellow and green braiding. (18)

In its ceremonial form the baby carrier is probably the most spectacular and ritually significant garment a woman possesses. It is also the most expensive because of enormous amounts of silver decorations stitched on over the needlework. A fully decorated baby carrier is worn by a bride and her attendants during the wedding ceremony and can be part of the bride price. It is used in other ceremonies such as the bridge ceremony which involves attempts to catch symbolic paper babies and flowers sent to protect and enrich the family paying for the ceremony. (9, 46)

CHILDREN'S GARMENTS

The Iu Mien believe in reincarnation, and babies are believed to be returned to earth from the spirit world. They need to be carefully cared for so that the ancestor spirits that sent them will not want to take them back. One of the ways to protect them is to have them wear colorful hats, *guh nguaaz-muoc*, which are believed to make the children look like flowers and thus deceive these ancestor flower spirits. (34, 35)

The boy's hat is made of triangular shaped red and black sections sewn together to form a beanie. Appliqué designs are sewn over these sections and edged with white braiding. An embroidered band circles the bottom edge. Traditionally, a common embroidery pattern used was *m'zuv huaa*, a Chinese word referring to a flower. This pattern, done in cross-stitch with white thread is also commonly used on the man's triangular head covering. (42) Tiger claws, *nda'maauh nyiuv*, is another common embroidery design used on a baby boy's hat. A red pompom is placed on the top and at the sides of the hat. Round silver discs are also sewn on, and there are other silver decorations and amulets attached to the top.

m'zuv huaa
m'zuv flower (ripples, waves)

nda'maauh nyiuv
tiger claw

The girl's hat is made from a wide embroidered band of fabric which is sewn together at the ends and gathered up on the long side to form the crown. Traditional designs used were the white grid-stitch patterns *som* and *lomh zeuv*. More recently these have been replaced by dense, colorful cross-stitch designs. Today, instead of embroidering a new piece of fabric, some women cut a section from a pair of used cross-stitched pants, no longer in style, to make the baby girl's hat. A wool ruff, *mouc-guaan*, similar to that on the coat, encircles the gathering stitches on the top of the hat, and the hat is further decorated with silver, beads, pompoms, tassels, and amulets.

When a ceremony is held in the home to ask for protection for the baby, spirit money is folded up into a ball by the priest and tied onto the hat or other garment worn by the child. (18) When a tiny baby is taken out visiting or when any small child is taken on a long trip on foot, pieces of long green leaves such as grass, rice, or thatch are attached to the hat to guard the child from the outside spirits such as the tiger or the wind spirit.

Since it is proper for a Mien woman to have her head covered at all times, a Mien girl generally wears her baby hat until she learns how to wrap her own six yard turban. This is quite difficult and is sometimes not mastered until after she has become an accomplished embroiderer and has made herself a pair of fully embroidered pants.

A small, simple hat is made for new-born babies which they wear for one month, and a small embroidered and appliqued bib, *guh nguaaz zaanh doic,* is also sometimes made for small children.

EVERYDAY GARMENTS FOR MEN

The traditional garments for Mien men consist of pants, jacket, sash and a turban or French beret. (12) However, Laotian men, who are more likely than women to travel out of their isolated villages to neighboring villages and market towns, often prefer wearing clothes that don't single them out as hilltribesmen.

The jacket, *jangc dorn lui,* cut mainly from rectangular pieces of fabric, has in addition a triangular piece which crosses diagonally in front and fastens along the side seam with round silver buttons, *la'kaux-junh,* and looped buttonholes, *la'kaux-kuotv,* made from braid. (15) This diagonal front opening and the cuffs of the sleeves are edged with appliqued red, white, and black strips of fabric like that on women's coat sleeves. Sometimes an embroidered pocket and, occasionally, other embroidery designs are placed on the front of the jacket. (36)

The sash, *jangc dorn hlaang,* is cut on the diagonal, pieced and sewn to form pointed, folded ends. This is wrapped around the waist under the jacket with the embroidered ends hanging down in front. The traditional designs put on the sash are the *som* and *lomh zeuv,* and the edges of the pointed ends are finished with braiding and double rows of chain stitch *ziem.* (37) Modern men's sashes are in brighter colors than the older ones and often have borders of cross-stiching. (43)

Pants for Mien men, *jangc dorn houx,* are cut like women's pants but have no embroidery on them. Both the men's and women's pants have very wide waists in order to fold and tuck in front, sarong fashion.

Some older men still wear these garments every day even in the United States, especially the beret. They also occasionally wear a sleeveless padded jacket, *lui-gaeng,* often silk, with a row of closely spaced silver buttons and loop button holes down the front. The buttons, *nyaanh lengx la'kaux,* are made from old silver coins depicting French Indochine, East India Co., and Victoria the Queen on them and dates such as 1814, 1910, 1923, and 1937. (38)

The turban, *jangc m'nqorngv beu,* is seldom worn any more except by a groom and his attendants during the wedding ceremony. It is embroidered much like the woman's turban but with less embroidery, and the fabric is red. (41, 72)

RITUAL GARMENTS

Families with the means to do so sponsor a *guaax dang* ceremony when a young man receives his religious name and obtains the necessary prerequisites for performing certain ceremonies. For this important ceremony mothers and wives make new jackets and sashes for their sons and husbands. In addition, they make several special ceremonial garments which include a small triangular embroidered piece, *paax-junh,* and a long embroidered and tasseled band, *sen-daoh daai,* both worn around the head with the ends hanging down the back. (42, 43, 44)

The embroidery on the triangular piece often includes the old cross-stitched tiger claws and *m'zuv hwaa* designs and rows of *lomh zeuv* and *som* done in white thread.

nda'maauh nyiuv
tiger claws

m'zuv huaa
m'zuv flower (ripples, waves)

The tasseled band is frequently embroidered with *Luh Guon-louc, Luh Guon-yienx* or *faam-cing nqun,* comb of the *faam-cing* bird, all old cross-stitched designs refering to the realm of the gods. Although *Faam-Cing* are the three Taoist gods, ruling over the highest heaven, who appear in several of the religious paintings used by the Mien in ceremonies (39), the women embroiderers insist that this pattern refers to the comb of a bird of the same name and not to the gods in the paintings. *Yienx* is a small printing stamp used on certain kinds of spirit money. (47)

Luh Guon-yienx
spirit money stamp

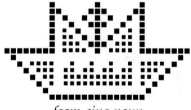

faam-cing nqun
comb of the *faam-cing* bird

The older bands frequently exhibit the old weave-stitch designs such as *da'jungh ndiangx, da'jungh* tree, which is the tree used to construct the bridge for bridge ceremonies connecting this world with the world of the gods. It is also used to make the stools for the *guaax dang* ceremony. Some of these old design names have been forgotten.

da'jungh ndiangx
da'jung tree

Old design with no known name
appearing on a *sen-daoh daai*

On recent versions of these garments, women embroider cross-stitch designs with the newer preferred colors replacing the old white, maroon, and black. (43) But some think that yellow should not be used for these ritual garments as it might cause vision problems for children or grandchildren.

A man also needs to have a ritual tunic, *lui-guaax,* (2, 3), and many-paneled skirt, *dun-junh* or *la'mienv junh.* (46) These two look distinctly Chinese, and some families possess heirlooms from China. New ones also can be ordered from China through relatives, although many women find suitable fabric, sometimes in Indian sari shops, in the United States. Lastly, a long black coat just like the woman's red ruffed coat is needed for the *guaax dang* initiate, and although it is acceptable to wear a coat belonging to a mother or wife, it is for this ceremony for sons and husbands that many of the new "women's" coats are now made in the United States. Higher merit-making ceremonies, quite rare, also require these religious garments. (40)

As white is important to the spirits, pieces of white cloth are attached somewhere to the clothing of both the men and their wives to let the spirits identify the participants in this ceremony. Men who have participated in this ceremony have a more elevated status and must take precautions not to endanger or contaminate themselves by walking beneath women's clothing, especially used pants.

An additional garment worn by priests while conducting ceremonies is the black, stiff hat made from woven human hair, *mba'biei-muoc.* The hat itself is bought from China and is then sometimes embellished with red pompoms and tassels like the baby girl's hat. (2, 3, 45)

WEDDING GARMENTS

Weddings require the participants to wear their newest, most ornate clothes and all of their silver jewelry. The women wear their ceremonial baby carriers displaying their wealth of silver decorations almost completely covering the needlework underneath and jingling as they move. (28, 29) Traditionally, the bride wore two sets of clothes. Ying Kwen says, "Many women still wear two sets of clothes when they marry so no one gets upset. One set made by her own family, her own thread, one the mother-in-law they give her to make that set. Both new." (53)

To her new home she takes a suitcase with gifts of clothes for her new mother-in-law and small gifts of embroidery for female relatives. These are often strips of embroidery for the coat neck facing, *lui-laeng,* but now are being replaced by cotton Thai sarongs. She also carries a quilted blanket made from black cloth filled with cotton batting. In California this is often replaced with Mexican wool blankets bought in flea markets. As she enters her in-laws' house, her new home, a pair of her mother-in-law's used pants is held over her head to insure her future obedience.

The groom wears a new outfit consisting of traditional pants, jacket, and sash. He also wears a red embroidered turban, and frequently wears silver jewelry, typically chain neck-laces and pendants. (41)

Wedding towels, *siqc jaauv-ndaauv,* are worn by the bride and groom and by the two attendants they each have. These are white rectangular cloths worn across the shoulder. They are embroidered at the ends with *lomh zeuv* and *som* designs like on a woman's turban. These designs are sometimes done in colored pairs to symbolize the couple. There is sometimes a central embroidery motif. The ends are hemmed and finished with braid. (4, 14, 41, 49) There are other, smaller towels given to the wedding guests at the washing ceremony, purchased ready-made, often of Chinese terry cloth with Chinese writing printed on them.

There are two types of Mien weddings, a small wedding lasting only one day and a big wedding lasting several days. For a big wedding, instead of a turban the bride must wear a unique wedding hat, a structure made from wood and bamboo fastened to the bride's head with bees' wax or black tape. (48) This supports the various pieces of fabric which make up her wedding hat. The fabric consists of a red square, an embroidered black square, and a long string of tassels forming a fringe.

The red square, *hongh mbiorngz*, is made from a piece of fabric, often wool purchased from the Chinese, which is edged with navy or black fabric and braid and trimmed at the corners with beads and red and white tassels. Occasionally, it is embellished with applique. (51) The beautifully embroidered rectanglar wedding cloth, *domh paax*, is made of black fabric which is marked out in rows by lines of stem- or chain-stitch. The spaces between the rows are filled with older variations of the *som* and *lomh zeuv* grid-stitch designs. The center often has some cross-stitch patterns such as *Luh Guon-louc*. This piece is also often decorated with red and white tassels at the four corners, red symbolizing baby boys and white, baby girls. (54, 56)

Central motif on a wedding square, *domh paax*

These two pieces are placed over the hat structure and the fringe, *zou-baaih,* is attached all around the edges so it hangs down in front of the bride's face. Mien legend says that the Mien are decended from a Chinese princess who was married to a dog hero. She wore a veil made of banana leaves so that she wouldn't see how ugly her husband was. (55) This veil or fringe is now made of red or maroon silk tassels strung onto a silver chain. On older fringes there were Chinese glass beads, both round, *zou,* and tubular, *zou-nzenc,* strung onto the top of the tassels, but these are now replaced with silver. Silver pendants, often with enameled designs, are also strung onto the silver chain.

During the wedding ceremony, bride and groom bow and kneel down many times to the priest, the ancestors, the parents, and the relatives as a mark of respect. A kneeling cloth or blanket, *zorx yoc,* is made for this purpose, and it is also used as a saddle blanket on the horse transporting the bride's father to the wedding ceremony in the village of the groom. It is also rectangular and is made from red Chinese fabric. It is bordered by a wide band of black cloth and the red central area is often decorated with black applique motifs edged with flat white finger braiding. (52)

In the ideal big wedding a bride used to wear three additional garments; white leggings, *la'baeng-baeqc,* white sash, *la'sin-baeqc,* and an additional black tasseled sash, *la'sin-congx.* The white leggings are embroidered with black thread in old weave-stitch designs such as the *da'jungh* tree, silver flower, and baby pig's hoof. (57, 58) Along most of its three to four yard length it is edged on one side by fish-bone embroidery, *mbiauz-mbungv*, which is not seen on any other garment and which very few women now know how to do.

mbiauz-mbungv
fish bone

nyaanh bingh
silver flower

The black tasseled sash, five to six yards long, also has on it some of the very oldest embroidery designs such as the *da'jungh* tree, baby pig's foot, spider, and the chipped or unfinished design, *ga'nyorc-nqaav*, all done in weave-stitch. The tassels on the ends are small pompoms attached to the ends of tightly twisted thread. This is wrapped around the waist of the bride over her other black sash. (59)

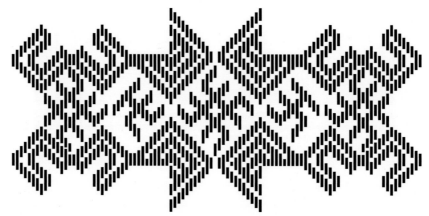

Group of designs often appearing on old pants and on the black sash. Includes *dungz-dorn deih*, baby pig's hoof, and *ga'nyorc-nqaav*, chipped, unfinished design. When some of the designs are done with black thread the grouping is called *ga'nyorc-jieqv*, black spider.

The white sash is narrower and somewhat shorter than the black one, and is done on finely woven white cotton with black weft shots or embroidery thread inserted at regular intervals. Black designs are embroidered between these stripes, and on some of these sashes the designs are similar to weave-stitch designs still used on the bottom of women's pants. This sash is worn on top of the tasseled sash. (58, 59)

These three garments, the two sashes and the leggings, are very rare now, and the white sash is often not recognized by Mien as a Mien garment.

When asked what a bride must make for her wedding, Mien women list most of the above garments. But when asked what they themselves actually made and wore, many were not able to comply with this ideal. Many families were too poor or too busy farming to allow a young girl the time or materials necessary to sew new bridal clothes. Most made the pants, but the standard for women's pants was much simpler in the past than the elaborately embroi-

44. Tasseled band worn by men while conducting religious ceremonies. This one is decorated with old weave-stitch designs. Cheng Wa Saetern, Oroville, California. SC

45. Hair hat worn by priest while conducting ceremonies. Made in China. Cheng Wa Saetern, Oroville, California. SC

46. Detail of priest's old silk religious skirt, probably made in China. A braided motif has been added on the bottom. Ann Goldman collection. AG

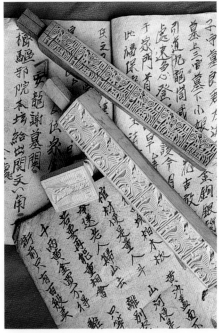

47. Wooden stamps used by Mien priests to print paper money and petitions to send, by burning, to the spirit world. The small one, Luh Guan-yienx, is represented by the embroidery design of the same name. Books, such as this one, are hand-written in Chinese on handmade bamboo paper. They record ceremonies, geneologies, astrological information, family histories, and traditional stories. It is to these Chinese characters that the design congx-nzaangc, refers. Ann Goldman collection. AG

48. Bride dressed for big three day, big-hat wedding. The wedding hat consists of an embroidered black square, a plain red square, and fringe covering a framework of bamboo and wood attached to the bride's head with bees' wax or black tape. Silver flower ornaments are pinned to the diagonal red band. Northern Thailand, 1960s. SL

49. Mien wedding, northern Thailand in the 1960s. Bride and attendants are wearing baby carriers in front like aprons in the Thai style. Apron bands are covered with bands of Hmong appliqued squares. SL

50. Women wearing traditional Mien clothing for the washing ceremony at a wedding, San Pablo, California. 1992. AG

51. *The red square, part of the bride's big wedding hat, is occasionally decorated with appliquéd designs. Oroville, California. SC*

52. *Kneeling cloth used at Mien weddings by the bridal couple during the long kneeling ceremony to show respect to ancestors, priests, parents, and relatives. Moang Kouei Saechao, San Jose, California. SC*

53. *Although Seng Van cannot embroider nor did she wear two pairs of pants at her wedding as is traditional, her mother bought her a new pair from Thailand (left), and her mother-in-law made her another pair (right) as part of her wedding trousseau. Oakland, California. SC*

54. Old embroidered wedding square. Suwadee Salmon collection, Nan, Thailand. LD

55. Old wedding fringe offered for sale by Mien refugees in Chiang Kham Camp, Thailand. 1990. LD

56. Central part of embroidered wedding square and tasseled corner. Ann Goldman collection. AG

57. *Heirloom white leggings modeled and owned by Cheng Xiang Saechao. Oakland, California. SC*

58. *White leggings (both ends of one strip, left), and white embroidered sash (right). Wedding square is in the background. All probably over 60 years old. Ann Goldman collection. AG*

59. *Heirloom embroidered white and black sashes and purse for wrapping silver. These belonged to Moang Kuei Saechao's husband's grandmother who was born in the 1890s in China. She wore the sashes at her wedding. In the background is her photo taken about 1970 in Nam Thouei, Laos. SC*

60. *Manh Orn wearing Mien silver earrings in a northern Thai village. 1990. AG.*

61. *Silver flower pins given at weddings and silver flower embroidery design on a pair of pants. Ann Goldman collection. AG*

62. *Shoulder bag with pompoms, tassels, and appliqué. Cheng Xiang Saechao, Oakland, California. SC*

63. *Embroidery wrapper with contents: sample cloth, sewing supplies, and unfinished pants panel. This belonged to Muey Seng Chao's young sister-in-law who was killed leaving Laos about 1976. Richmond, California. AG*

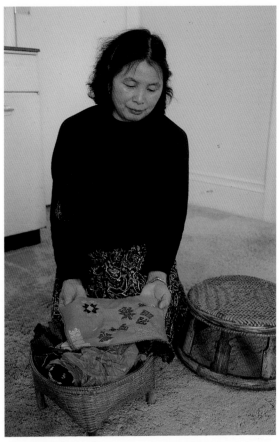

64. *Meuy Yoon Phan showing old weave-stitch designs she is saving on her sample cloth. Oakland, California. SC*

65. *Several sample cloths sewn together. Cheng Wa Saetern. Oroville, California. SC*

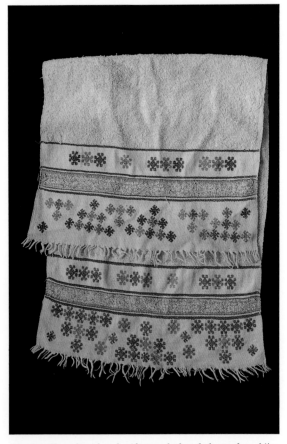

66. *Small embroidered gift towel that belonged to Yien Choy Saechao's mother. San Jose, California. SC*

67. *Boots with appliqué and tassels. Made by Manh Orn for her brother. Cheng Xiang Saechao. Oakland, California. SC*

68. Small purses made to sell or give as gifts. Some are made from old sashes or pants' panels. Ann Goldman collection. AG

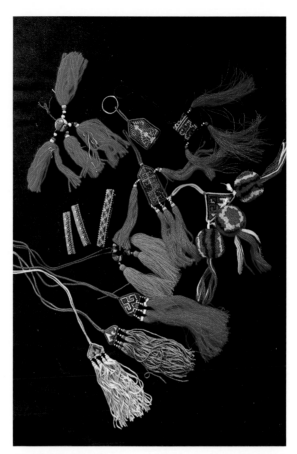

69. Ornaments, key fobs, necklases, and barrettes with embroidery, tassels, netting, and pompoms. Ann Goldman collection. AG

70. Neckties made by Muey Sio Fong. Richmond, California. AG

71. Scarves embroidered by Muey Sio Fong and her mother, Liw Chian Saechao. Ann Goldman collection. AG

72. *Mien man's turban, left, and Hmong woman's apron sash end showing similar designs. Ann Goldman collection. AG*

73. *Different regional color preferences on women's pants. Left, Nan/Sayabouri colors, center, Red Thai pants from Chiangrai Province, and right, northern Lao style. Ann Goldman collection. AG*

74. Mien women in Nan Province. 1990. Turbans are wrapped flat around the head with the embroidered ends sticking out at the top. AG

75. Mien pants, Nan Province, Thailand. 1990. Designs formerly done with white thread are now done in blue. AG collection. AG

77. Detail of Vietnamese Yao coat tail designs. Lois Callaway collection. SC

76. Vietnamese Yao with embroidered coat tails and leg cuffs. 1960s. SL

78. Turban ends made in Sayabouri Province, Laos. Torn Chan Saephan, Oroville, California. AG

79. Northern Laos style pants (left). Yen Meng Saephan, Nam Kueng, Laos, 1970s. Chiangrai style (right) with possible influence from Nan, Phayao, or Sayabouri Provinces. Ann Goldman collection. AG

80. Bottom edge of pant legs showing difference between northern Lao pants with an added gusset and Thai pants without the gusset. Ann Goldman collection. AG

81. Chiangrai Mien use a red dye for their pants that frequently runs. Northern Thai village, 1990. AG

82. Pants made in Sayabouri Province, Laos, in the 1970s by Cheng Wa Saetern. Oroville, California. SC

83. Pants purchased in a Mien village near Luang Prabang, Laos, in 1968. Very similar to Sayabouri pants (82) in color and some design elements but has leg gusset and sopc biangh border design like Mien from Namtha area. Jack Kornfield collection. AG

84. *Mien women in a village in northern Thailand wearing pants from various regions. From left, pants represent styles from Chiangrai Province, northern Laos, Nan Province, Chiangrai Province, and the United States. 1990. LD*

85. *Older woman in Nan Province preparing food for New Year. She wears new pants but they are the easy, spaced, weave-stitch style. 1990. AG*

86. *Detail of pants (81). All designs are spaced and done in weave-stitch. AG*

87. Planting dry rice in northern Thailand. 1960s. SL

88. Women making paper in Laos. 1960s. The bamboo pulp is poured onto cloth racks to dry. 1960s. SL

89. Feuy Tong Saeyang's pants patched with a practice piece done by her daughter when she was about four. Made in Chiang Kham, Thailand. 1980s. AG

90. Two pairs of pants made in northern Laos, probably in the 1960s, by Cheng Xiang Saechao showing increasing amounts of embroidery and closer spacing of the designs. Oakland, California. SC

91. Muey Sio Fong's wedding pants made in Nam Thouei, Laos, 1970. These have alternating rows of white grid-stitch designs and new cross-stitch designs. At the time, this style was considered very new and beautiful. AG

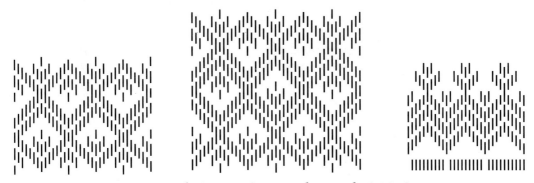

Weave stitch designs from a white sash, *la'sin-baeqc.*

dered ones of today. Meuy Yoon says, "When my mother was young, everybody did pants the same. Same design, same color. Some did darker, some lighter, that's all. Special pants for weddings were not very different, just smaller (weave) material. If they're rich people they use silk thread. If not rich, they use half silk. Only the colored thread is silk, the white not silk. My parents were not too poor, I got silk."

Even when they were able to take a year off from field work to prepare for the wedding, they seldom made all the garments for a big wedding themselves but instead borrowed some or did without. Brides whose mothers had had big weddings were more likely to be given big weddings, and often the rarer garments were passed down by a grandmother or great-grandmother. As these garments wore out, were lost, discarded, or sold during the migration south, they were not replaced, and few families have access to them any more.

ACCESSORIES, DECORATIONS, GIFTS

Many families have flat purses, *nyaanh beu,* that have been in their families for generations. (59) These were used to carry silver or money and could be rolled up or folded and tucked into the waist sash. These purses are square and made of three layers of fabric sewn together at the edges but left open at one corner. The purse is trimmed with braid which also forms a loop closure and cord for wrapping around the purse. The embroidery on the top layer exhibits, according to many people, the oldest use of the cross-stitch designs. These designs usually include the tiger claw design.

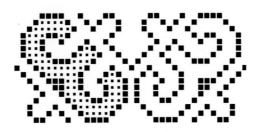

nda'maauh nyiuv
tiger claw

Women use a larger shoulder bag, *mbuoqc jorngx,* made from narrow bands of hand-loomed striped fabric, one long piece forming the shoulder strap with a shorter piece forming the central body of the bag. This is decorated with elongated pompoms, *jorngx-guaan,* and appliqué designs edged with flat braiding. (62) Smaller purses with drawstrings, *mbuoqc hlopv,* quite plain or solidly embroidered and trimmed with appliquéd strips and tassels are used for storing seed and small valuables.

As protection from morning chill and from mosquitoes, women sometimes wrap long, thin indigo-dyed bands of fabric, *la'baeng,* around their lower legs.

Mien women living in the mountains of Thailand and Laos work hard all day and seldom have much spare time. Any extra time they can squeeze out of the day is spent embroidering. Therefore, some embroidery supplies and work in progress are carried with them in an embroidery wrapper, *congx-beu*. This wrapper is a square of cloth, edged with braiding, often with a pocket sewn onto it to hold small things like thread or beads. It is decorated with some embroidery at the corners, and often serves also as a sample cloth. When working on a garment, like a panel for a pair of pants, the parts not being worked on are carefully wrapped in cloth to keep them clean. This neat bundle is then wrapped in the embroidery wrapper which is then folded and put in the sewing basket, carried in the shoulder bag, or tied around the waist like a fanny pack. (63)

Scraps of fabric used as sample cloths, *congx-buonv*, are also carried in the wrapper. These are used to record new designs or parts of designs a woman sees on someone else's clothes and might want to use on her own pants later on. Often these are new cross-stitch designs, but women also copy down the very old designs, the ones seldom used now, in an attempt to save them from extinction. They hope to make themselves a pair of pants using the old designs so that when they die and are buried in these pants, the ancestor spirits will recognize them and know they preserved the culture. (64, 65)

Silk or wool yarn tassels, *nyueic* or *nqingh nqou*, and pompoms, *guaan*, mostly red, are used to embellish the woman's coat, baby hats, baby carriers, purses, and various ceremonial and decorative items. (33, 43, 106)

Silver jewelry, often embellished with braid and tassels, is used extensively, especially on ceremonial occasions. Silver buttons and ornaments are sewn directly onto garments like men's jackets, baby hats, and baby carriers. (15, 19, 35) Skilled silversmiths in the United States, Thailand, and Laos fashion small silver earrings, *m'normh hiun*, (60), and bracelets, *buoz-jiemh*, which are worn daily, and elaborate pendants and chains worn during big ceremonies when a woman wishes to display her wealth. A bride might wear many pounds of silver, mostly on her baby carrier. (29, 50) To the back of her coat under the ruff she attaches a *hlaang-mbiorngc* consisting of long strands of braid wrapped in silver with tassels or silver bells on the ends. Also hanging down her back, and jingling as she moves, is an elaborate piece of jewelry, *ba'finx*, with Chinese glass beads, silver chains, enameled fish and flowers, and amulets in the shape of pestles, fish, sesame seeds, scissors, tweezers, and the like. (28) There are also long chains of silver, *m'nqorngv-limc*, which are wrapped diagonally around the turban. Around her neck a Mien woman displays her *jaang-waanh*, which is a thick heavy silver necklace, and down the front opening of her coat she has several decorated rectangular silver buckles, *la'kaux-mbeih*. The bridal couple is often given gifts of flattened silver sheets cut into shapes of trees and flowers, *nyaanh biangh*, and mounted on long silver pins which can be stuck into the turban, wedding towel, or special red band. (48, 61)

As with the garments, the styles of many of these decorations have changed over the years, the trend being to replace the silk tassels with synthetic material and to replace the old Chinese glass beads with more and more silver.

Some embroidered items are made simply as gifts to show interest in or gratitude to another person. An old custom was for a girl to embroider the ends of a small towel, *siqc jaauv-baeqc*, for her boyfriend. (66) She could have someone write a song in Chinese to send to the boy with the towel. These towels were often of Chinese terry cloth with either Chinese characters or English messages such as "Good morning" printed on them. They were worn around the necks of men with the embroidered ends in front. Girls also used small towels at the back of the waist tucked into the sash at each side to hold down the long tassels on the coat decorations so they wouldn't get entangled. This type of small towel is also held in the groom's hands at the wedding during the bowing ceremony.

Boots, *heh tongv*, are now rare. The one pair seen in California was given as a gift in gratitude for help given in the past. Made in Laos in the 1950s, they were used by a priest during ceremonies. They are made of heavy, white cotton fabric and decorated with red appliqué, braid, and tassels. (67)

People who have worked with the Mien in Thailand or in the United States are also given gifts of embroidery. These take the form of tasseled decorations, purses, spectacle holders, scarves, and the like. (68, 69, 71)

At important American and Mien events in the United States young Mien men often wear beautifully embroidered neckties made by their wives or mothers. (70) Some women make westernized skirts decorated with Mien embroidery designs and elegant handbags from embroidered pants' panels.

Cross-stitch design fragments used on tassels.

Sopc-biangh or squash flower variation on the bottom border of a woman's pants.

REGIONAL DIFFERENCES

Mien have shared traditional designs with other hilltribe groups for generations, (72), and close contact with the Hmong in particular has provided opportunities for appreciation and exchange of embroidery patterns. (49) However, the dramatic changes in designs, colors, density, and materials that have occurred in Mien embroidery since about 1960 seem to be due mostly to increased leisure time in refugee centers, greater availability of supplies, and to renewed contact with other groups of Lao Mien also forced to flee south because of war. Once in Thailand they often lived with Mien who had entered Thailand years before. These different groups of Mien had developed distinctive embroidery styles. (73)

Mien migrated into Nan and Phayao Provinces in Thailand from Sayabouri Province in Laos from a hundred to a hundred and fifty years ago. In both of these areas women still use a predominence of red, yellow or orange, and white thread in their embroidery, although they are now replacing white thread with blue. (75) They have long turbans, embroidered on the ends, which they wrap flat around their heads with the embroidered part sticking up, sometimes causing them to be referred to as deer head, deer horns, or big head Mien. (74, 100) Perhaps the Sayabouri Mien migrated southwest from northern Vietnam where Mien in the 1960s were also wearing black clothes with red, yellow, and white embroidery. Vietnamese Mien women's pants were embroidered at the bottom with designs similar to those used by Lao Mien. (76) On the women's coat tails was a bird motif somewhat like one later used by Mien in Thailand on men's jackets and on squares made in the refugee camps for sale to outsiders. (77)

The Phayao and Nan Mien and also those from Sayabouri and Luang Prabang Provinces in Laos were already using some cross-stitch designs on their pants by the 1960s when Mien began to move south out of Namtha Province. (82, 83)

In the 1940s during Second World War, Mien migrated out of the northwest of Laos into Chiangrai Province in Thailand. These Mien used large amounts of white thread in their embroidery with smaller amounts of maroon, yellow, and dark indigo, but as they moved south into Thailand they increased the amount of maroon or magenta used. This particular Thai dye was often not fast and resulted in giving the pants a distinct all-over red color. Due to this, these Mien were often referred to as the red Mien by later migrants. (81) Over the years the Chiangrai Mien intermingled with neighboring Mien in Phayao and Nan Provinces, borrowing some of their cross-stitch designs and color combinations to put on their pants. (79)

In contrast to Mien who have migrated south from the relatively isolated Namtha area since the 1960s, most Mien who migrated into Thailand earlier do not use an embroidered gusset on

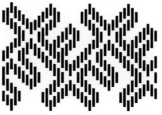

congx-ceix
spike embroidery

23

their pants legs, and they don't embroider the rows on their pants out to the edge of the panel since that part doesn't show when worn. (80, 82) On the bottom of their pants, these earlier migrants still prefer the variation of the weave-stitch, which they call *congx-ceix*, considered the oldest of the three variations.

In addition, as dividers between embroidered sections on the pants, Namtha Mien tend to put rows of stem-stitch, *njiuc*, on only one side of the saw-tooth design, *njoux*, instead of on both sides like the Thai and Sayabouri Mien, who also tend to make the sawtooth design larger. (79)

Namtha Mien: *njoux, njiuc*
Sawtooth, stem

Thai Mien: *njiuc, njoux, njiuc*
stitch Stem stitch, sawtooth, stem stitch

In the spider section, Thai Mien tend to use double rows of grid-stitch in designs in which the Namtha Mien use single rows.

Namtha Mien: single row

Thai Mien: double row

On their pants, Thai Mien tend to embroider different colored *som* designs in the same row, but the Namtha Mien almost always embroider the whole row of *som* design in white, or more recently in blue.

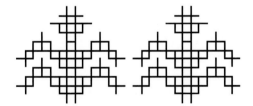

Namtha Mien: *Som* all one color

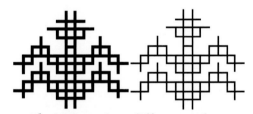

Thai Mien: *Som* different colors

The current migration of Namtha Mien to Thailand began in the 1970s. At the time of migration they used mostly white, maroon, yellow, and green embroidery, with white pre-dominating. They are sometimes jokingly called cabbage head people because they wrap their turbans diagonally around their heads. In addition to the embroidery on the ends of the turbans, they have added a row of designs in the center section which shows when worn. They construct their pants a bit differently by adding an extra piece or gusset, *houx-caamv*, at the bottom edge, and now they all prefer to use *sopc biangh*, pumpkin flower, on the bottom weave-stitch section.

sopc biangh
pumpkin blossom

Other areas of Laos show combinations of these features. Pants collected near Luang Prabang in 1968 have a very large gusset piece, *sopc biangh* embroidery, and stem-stitch on only one side of the large sawtooth design. (83)

In certain Thai Mien villages on the migration route near the Mekong River one finds Mien from all these different areas. Most of them were born elsewhere and settled in these villages when forced out of their own villages in Laos and Thailand because of war. Their pants often reflect their areas of origin. Mien women from Phayao Province have red, yellow, and white designs on their pants, women from Chiangrai Province have large amounts of magenta in their embroidery designs while newer arrivals from Laos use embroidery with more white. Many have now been resettled in the United States, Canada, and France, and their relatives remaining in the Thai villages are beginning to wear pants reflecting the color preferences of the Western Mien which are blue, yellow, and dark maroon. (84)

Mien women in a literacy class in the early 1960s. Northern Thailand. Photo by Sylvia Lombard.

Grid-stitch *ga'nyorc* or spider section of embroidery on a pair of woman's pants.

MIGRATION

FROM LAOS TO AMERICA

The effect of migration on the lives of the Mien has been significant. Great numbers of Mien have traveled from small, isolated, self-sufficient villages with no schools, stores, hospitals, electricity, communication, or transportation systems to the the vast and complicated urban settings of California and Oregon. The adjustments necessary to cope with change and new situations began when families were routed out of their mountain villages and told to flee because of war. The story of these changes is told by several Mien women: Liw Chian Saechao and her daughter Muey Sio Fong, Ying Kwen Saeteun, Toud Kouei Law, Muey Seng Chao, Liew Sieng Saeteun, and Meuy Yoon Phan.

Liw Chian, who is the oldest, begins, "My parents were both born in China and moved to Moung Noi, Laos, before they were married. I was born in Moung Noi in 1931, one of nine children. In my village there were only nine or ten families. Almost everyone was related to my father's or my mother's side.

"The house was made of posts made from big trees. Small wood is put through the holes in the big posts. In Laos they don't have measuring tape, measure by their hands. *Buoz-camh* is the distance of your out-stretched arms. Finger to finger. Big house is nine, eight, or seven *buoz-camh* wide. Some families have twenty people and seven poles. Our house had four poles and ten or more people.

"The children all played together. We made little houses. We pretended little white flowers were rice and we tied them together and hung them up on rice drying racks. The boys made wood horses with wheels to pull. And they played with stilts, *maaz-gaqc*. We had races and played hide and seek in the grass. In my family we got to play sometimes, but not too much because my father was too busy and wanted us to work.

"At that time we only farmed on the mountains, not lowland. We lived a long time in Moung Noi and the land was all used up so we had to move to new land in Moung Nang.

"Moung Sing was the big market town. It took all day to walk there. Only the men went to buy salt and different things. Children and women usually didn't go. If they went, they would get sick when they came back. "Once a year Chinese traders came through our village. They brought big heavy black metal cooking pots, plant medicine, yarn for the coats, dye, white fabric, and beads. Lahu people made cotton thread and brought it to the village to sell. Silk came from Namtha. Tai Dam people made it and traders came to sell.

"My first pair of pants my sister made for me. She put *congx-sieqv* on the bottom. She said, 'If you want to wear (pants), you have to learn to embroider to have more.' My mother was

congx-sieqc
little girl embroidery

very busy. She had to dye cloth, make paper, care for kids, work on the farm. In one year she could just make one pair pants with only weave-stitch." (85, 86)

"My mother taught me to embroider. She would embroider one design and I would have to copy it and count the threads. We didn't have school, didn't have to work in the fields, we just took care of younger brothers and sisters. We couldn't wait for younger children to go to sleep so we could learn to do embroidery.

"When I was seven or eight, I made my own pair of pants. On the bottom it had *Wuanh Guangv congx* and two grid-stitch rows (*som*). And then *jienv* (gibbon). Then one *lomh zeuv* and two *som*. "

Wuonh Guangv congx
Wuonh Guangv embroidery

jienv
gibbon

Other women told similar stories of their childhood. Muey Seng who was born in Moung Sai says, "I remember playing with my older brother. Sometime when my mom went to the fields, we went together. We helped my parents. We had to take care of my young brother, we had to cut the leaves in the field, we planted the rice and corn. We had to take up the weeds. When we went home, we had to carry my brother.

"Playing with my brother, we would go outside, we cut the grass and banana tree, and made a little house, and we stayed there. We took the banana leaves to make the clothes. Tear in strips and make a skirt. Sometimes we would make Mien tassels out of banana leaves for a jacket. My brother made shoes for me from the wood. He would take the wood, and he cut, and he took the drill, made the hole, and he took the root to tie it. He was seven or eight."

Liw Chian continues, "When I was old enough, I worked in the fields like my parents. The hardest farm work is the first clearing of the field from January to March. Then burn in early May. To plant, the men make the hole with a stick, and the women drop the seeds in. You always have to go in pairs. Start at the bottom of the field. All together, go up the hill. The man has to walk backwards. Women follow them. (87)

"I helped my mother dye cloth. When dry, put it in the dye. Take out, dry, dye again. I helped make paper. When young bamboo come out and get tall, you cut down and cut between the sections. Cut out the joints, peel the skin and peel out the inside. Just use a little bit. Take home and boil with white powder. Later rinse, rinse, rinse, then put in a basket and leave until soft. One or one and one half months. Then beat it on a chopping block. Put in water and pick out the big chunks. Pour out on screen made from a square of fabric stretched on a wood frame. Let it dry awhile. Make three hundred to six hundred pieces each year. When dry, peel off and fold very carefully and put aside. Has to be young bamboo. Cook many batches. (88) Use big kettles we buy from Chinese. Paper used for books and spirit money. Also for wrapping things like dried vegetables. Mostly for ceremonies. (47)

"Very, very poor people might not have a paper frame. Wait until other people are finished with their frame, then borrow it. Families might let them use their extra pulp if they don't need. Poor, poor people can't have many ceremonies."

Meuy Yoon born in 1940 says, "We had a big, big farm. My father wanted all the family to work hard. They paid another woman to do embroidery for me. She had no husband and she was poor so she helped people a lot.

"I was nine years when I started my own pants, but it wasn't my mother who taught me. She cut the material and found the thread for me. She said, 'I don't have time to teach you. Can you take to your friend to teach you?' I went out to take care of the cows and my friend taught me. She was eleven years old. We went very early in the morning and took the cows out of the pen to where there is grass to eat. Thirty-two cows. If the cows run to a different place, we have to follow them.

"Boys just played. They would go to the river and catch fish. Or if it was very hot they would take banana trees and make a raft for swimming on the river. We did it too. Sometimes when we went to the river to swim, when we got out we couldn't find some of the cows. Sometimes we sang. When you're out with the cows you can sing by yourself if you're lonely, or you can sing to a friend who is farther away.

"We stayed all day. We just took rice and some salt and chili pepper for lunch. We didn't have much. Sometimes we made a fire. We could find banana blossoms to eat. We knew how to do it. My friend who taught me embroidery she was very nice. She knew how to do a lot and we did them together. We learned how to do embroidery all day if the cows stayed good.

"*Wuanh Guangv congx* was what I used on the first and second pair of pants. The first pair was all weave-stitch, *congx-sieqv*. The only other stitch was *njiu-njiuc* (stem-stitch). The second pair had grid-stitch, too.

"Each year girls have to learn new designs so they can make grown up pants. We look at people with nice pants and everyone wants to learn to make nice pants. Usually men don't know the names of the patterns. They didn't do it. Women don't write, men don't do embroidery. If a woman works hard her husband doesn't say anything about her embroidery, but if she's lazy he might say, 'Why don't you learn new things, new stitches?'"

Liw Chian continues, "I got married at ninteen years old. It was a small wedding. We just killed one pig so the village people would know we were married. I didn't make any special things for the wedding.

"Later, people, Laotian leaders came to our village to ask the village leaders for Mien soldiers. We didn't know why they needed soldiers. Our village leader picked one person and gave to them.

"Then, late one night we heard an airplane and saw its light in the sky. We were very scared because we didn't know what it was. We had heard that airplanes could come and drop bombs on the village and everybody would die. "After that soldiers often come to village, and families began to move things out to the jungle and farms to hide them because they were afraid soldiers would take them. First they would come and ask for rice. Everyone had to give some rice. Then they asked for chickens to eat. Later they asked for pigs. Then cows. They would just point to the cow they wanted and the people had to kill it for them to eat.

"When we left, we took clothing, money, food, pots for cooking. We had four children then. My husband and I each carried one child. Muey Sio and her brother walked. We had two horses that carried clothes, blankets, rice, small pots. Now I have nothing I had then, except three children, one pair of pants, one pair earrings, and one silver necklace."

Muey Sio, her daughter, who was about seven at that time recalls, "I remember the year we had to move, my mother said, 'We work very hard, but this year probably we will not get to eat this food.' She was right. In April 1962 we moved to another village at night. We could hear guns far away.

"We moved three times. The first time not too far from the village, and we stayed until the communists saw us there. Then across the river where we stayed two, three months. But they were shooting too much at night again so we moved way, way up on the mountain to Nam He Bong. We had to carry what we ate and when that was gone we had to sneak back to our farm for more food.

"I remember there was an old, old woman who stayed on our farm to take care of our animals. When we went back to kill a pig to take to the jungle we saw her there. Very sad. She was very old and maybe handicapped, and we could not take her. She cried and cried. We told her that was the last time we could go back. That was the last time we saw her.

"We built little houses of banana leaves and bamboo. We got different things to eat in the jungle. It was very dangerous there. One day they threw a bomb to the field and many people were hurt.

"From there we went to Nam Woua where the airplanes flew over and dropped rice. We stayed outside the village with many, many people from different villages. They all came together there. There were a lot of soldiers in uniform there and people with big jobs and walkie-talkies. We stayed there a few weeks and then walked to Nam Thouei."

Nam Thouei was a large area where refugees from northern Laos congregated after being forced from their villages. It was next to Nam Yu which was a military base and had air strips.

Toud Kuei's family went to Nam Woua about the same time. She says, "Laotians spent all their money moving. Seven, eight, nine, ten years moving. People with no money had to stay there with the communists. In Nam Woua and Nam Thouei rice was supplied for new people until they could grow some. They also gave bread and some vegetables. French bread. We never had before and no one liked it. We cooked it for the pigs, they liked it. There were many Hmong and different people. You could not talk to them. There were also government people, Americans, French. Different people spoke funny, they talked like ducks!"

Muey Sio continues, "We went to Nam Thouei probably in 1963. Many people went there and built their villages. Each village picked its own place to build. It's not very good for the Mien people to move to new villages like that. We don't know how to control the spirits if we do like that. That's why many people got sick and died.

"I remember my uncles learning to read and write Chinese characters from my grandfather. There are two fires in Mien houses. Men always sit at their fire and the women sit at the kitchen fire. Girls could listen to the Chinese lessons, and we could remember what we heard, but we didn't go over there to look so we could not see the letters. Only the boys learned to write. It never happened in our country that a girl wanted to learn to write Chinese. Boys never did embroidery. That's not their job.

"I must have learned to use a needle when I was about seven years old in Moung Nang. Before, I tried to use the needle a little bit, but I was just playing and I didn't know how to do the designs. (89) My mother taught me to embroider. When I learned, she taught two or three children, my cousins. She never got mad. I sat down, my mom sat down, they all sat down and wanted her to teach them. Me and my cousins we all wanted to race. My cousins thought I could embroider and get new pants to wear and they wouldn't get any. I embroidered my first pair of pants in Nam Thouei. First I did the bottom rows of weave-stitch, the *sopc biangh* pattern. I never learned *Wuonh Guangv* stitch which my mother used when she was young. I just used red, black, green, yellow, and white thread. At that time we didn't use (royal) blue yet."

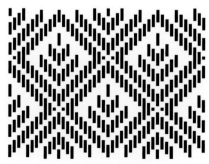

sopc biangh
pumpkin blossom

"In Nam Thouei people started putting the old designs closer together. I think my third or fourth pair were like that. But we had to work all the time so the everyday pants were just the old kind that took less time. (90)

"When I walked around Nam Thouei, I could see other kinds of embroidery on women's pants, especially the cross-stitch. Not too many people did that stitch on their pants. Only the people from other places. When I first saw it it looked very different with many, many colors. You need many colors with the cross-stitch or you can't do the patterns. But parents don't want you to change style. In our village we changed very slow. My uncle was the leader and he didn't want his village people to change too much. He said, 'No, we cannot change like that. That's very different. That's not like us.' He was talking about the embroidery, the clothes.

"The older people have a story. If you are too young when you do the cross-stitch, it will cross your heart and you cannot think, you can't do anything and you're not so smart. They believe that. There is cross-stitch on the collar of the coat, and everyone has to do that, but I remember my grandmother said, 'You're too young, don't embroider that yet. I'll help you.' I saw some people doing cross-stitching. I remember I copied the tiger claw and that zig-zag design to put on my pants, but my aunt saw it and she said, 'You're too young. Don't do that embroidery on this pair of pants yet. The next pants you can do it, but not on this pair.'"

nda'maauh nyiuv
tiger claw

jung hungh
dragon, or rainbow

"I taught my grandmother the grid-stitch in 1969 or 1970. She wanted to learn the new stitch. It was fun to teach my grandmother.

"I was nineteen or twenty when I got married. After we got engaged, I had one year to embroider for my wedding. I didn't have to do field work that year because I had to do so much embroidery. For myself I had to make one pair of pants, one sash, and one turban. I also had to make one pair of pants for my mother-in-law.

"My wedding pants were the first ones I used cross-stitch on. I used pearl cotton for the first time on my wedding pants. There was a little market in Nam Thouei run by Chinese, Lao and Lay people. You could buy it there. You spent every spare moment embroidering. When men sleep, women embroider. You take everywhere to do when you have ten spare minutes."

janx-gekv tei, janx-taiv biauv
Chinese stairs, Thai houses

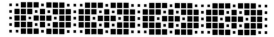

nda'maauh nyiuv
tiger claws

Muey Sio's wedding pants have alternating rows of the new cross-stitch designs and the old *som* design done in grid-stitch. (91) Many women did transitional pants in rows like this in the early 1970s when women were first putting cross-stitch on their pants. They thought they were very beautiful, and many women refer to them as "A number One" pants or "the most beautiful pants of 1972".

Muey Sio continues, "In January 1972 we had to leave Nam Thouei. On New Year's Day. The communists came running into the village shooting guns. Hundreds of people all moved in different directions into the jungle. We didn't have time to pack. I took the old clothes I was

jouv coix biangh
chive flower

faam-cing dueiv
tail of *famh cing* bird

wearing and my new clothes and a few pieces of jewelry my Mom gave me for my wedding. And food to eat. And we had to carry the children, too. We had to leave a lot. We just walked out the door and went.

"We moved down to Houei Orh (on the Mekong River) with six to ten other Mien families."

Muey Seng's family moved directly from their village in northern Laos south to the Mekong River in the early 1960s. "We left Moung Sai because there was no place to make a field. There were soldiers. I think I was eight years. The whole village couldn't stay there because the communists they came over. Every week they came and they wanted people to work for them, to carry food, bombs, or they needed soldiers. My father, people who had the horse, had to go with them, to bring the things. After about one and a half weeks they can come home. They didn't pay anything. If we don't do it, it's against the law. They can do something to you."

Muey Yoon and her family also moved down to Nam Kueng on the Mekong River in the mid 1960s. "We copied cross-stitch in Nam Kueng. I still have one pair of pants I made there. Thai Mien were there and they used cross-stitch. Young people changed their embroidery a lot, but the old people don't want to change. Not so much. Just a few cross-stitch designs. Some parents object to young girls changing but everyone wants to copy the new designs. That time cross-stitch on pants only. Not waist sash or turban. They use designs on pants that looked kind of like the horns on Thai houses. In Nam Kueng people still didn't do much cross-stitch because we were still working hard. In Nam Kueng I learned *sopc biangh* pattern from my cousin. I remember her daughter said, 'You are already big. Why are you learning?' People who came from Namtha (near the city) mostly had *sopc biangh*. People from my place all have *Wuanh Guangv congx*."

janx-gekv (taiv) tei (biauv)
Chinese (or Thai) stairs (or houses)

Ying Kwen was nine when she moved to Nam Kueng in 1966, and she recalls, "In Nam Kueng each leader was told they had to send boys and girls to school. If they weren't told they had to send girls, they wouldn't. My grand-father was village leader and he signed me up. I didn't really want to go. You know Mien people say, 'You want to be lazy and go to school? You don't want to work on the farm? You don't want to do embroidery and learn how to make clothes? By the time you finish high school when you come home, you cannot cook, you cannot embroider. Nobody will want to marry you, and when you come in the village you'll have to carry the cane. You can't walk anymore. Too old you can't do anything.'

"When I studied all the other girls at school wore uniforms. I didn't at first because I was afraid to take my turban and earrings off. You had to buy the uniform, and I didn't have money. I was a good student, first every month, so there was no problem with books. They give you five books for first prize and one case of pencils. But they didn't pay for clothes. I had to help my cousin embroider so she paid me some money, and I worked for my aunts and uncles. So I saved up and bought one uniform sarong.

"I went to school five years. I finished high school. I didn't wear Mien at all, not anywhere. On the farm I wore long sarong and blouse. At school I wore a white blouse and uniform skirt. Just walking along the road I looked like any other Lao person. I graduated in May 1975, and I went to Thailand in July."

Muey Sio says, "In 1975 many communists came and stayed in our village, and they changed the rules. Nobody liked what they wanted, what they did. They said they wanted all the people in the village to make the farm, grow food and animals and put it all together. You could grow things, but if other people didn't have you had to share. For the older people, they wouldn't let them stay in their own houses and take care of the grandchildren. They were just scared, so they moved. Many people moved in 1975."

Crossing the Mekong River was risky. It was usually done at night. Sometimes boats capsized and people drowned. Often people were shot at. One woman says her family crossed on a raft made from tires bound together. She carried many things including six pairs of pants. The raft fell apart, and people had to grab hold of the tires. But everything else fell in. Clothes, money, gold, everything.

Another woman wore three pairs of pants when she escaped. "If the communists see you have a lot of clothes they know you are leaving and you never go back."

One woman's family went to Thailand via Burma where they lived with Burmese Mien people. "We didn't live there a long time so didn't have to learn their designs. Also too busy working there. They use material that looks so funny, not so nice. Bigger weave and a little yellow. Not the same designs. I left all my things in Burma."

When the refugee camps were first established in Thailand, provisions were minimal. People had to build shelters with whatever materials were at hand, food was scarce and there was much sickness. Muey Yoon recalls, "We built tiny little houses, like tents. My daughter, me, and my aunt. My husband died in Nam Kueng. I had one adopted daughter. She was thirteen years old. She could cook and do everything. We moved to a new place, no medicine. She had diarrhea for one day and she died. Old people, young people they die a lot in Chiang Khong Camp. But Mien people don't die as many as Lahu people. I don't know why. And my daughter was Lahu."

During the same years that the Lao Mien were fleeing south to escape war, Mien and other hilltribe people in Thailand were being evacuated out of the mountains along the Lao border and put into resettlement areas. Many were destitute and there was little help for them.

In order to offer some assistance, missionaries working in that area began to buy their needlework and then to develop markets for their embroidery. Efforts were made to influence the colors and the designs in order to make them more desirable in the Western market. A search was made for colorfast materials. A beautiful colorfast bright blue thread was introduced which many Mien began to use on their own clothes. Japanese embroidery pattern books were introduced. Women's clubs in Bangkok began to host talks on the plight of the hilltribes and on their embroidery. Women whose husbands were working for USAID, United States Aid for International Development, in Laos became interested in starting similar projects there. Lois Callaway, an American missionary in northern Thailand, was instrumental in the development and marketing of embroidered products. When the refugee camps were established in northern Thailand, the government allowed her established marketing project to work inside the camps. Many Mien women who passed through those camps speak of the oportunity they had to earn cash by doing embroidery for her project.

Of the camp Muey Sio says, "It was very hard to get any money in that camp. Thai people came into the camp and hired people to go work in the tobacco factory. But too many people wanted to go. Also, I had a tiny baby then and my husband was sick for many months, so I stayed in the camp and did embroidery for the outside people. You could work all day and do a small embroidered square for three and a half or four baht, and sometimes they didn't even pay you. The Callaways paid more, but not everyone could get their work. I only got their work twice."

Ying Kwen adds, "We did squares and wall hangings and bands. They provided all the colors. Sometimes I liked the colors and sometimes not. We got five baht, ten baht, fifteen baht, sixty baht." (94)

Most of the design samples were cross-stitch designs, and many were Thai Mien designs that were new to the Lao Mien. They liked them and copied them on their sample cloths and on their pants. The newly discovered ice blue was very popular and continued to replace white on women's pants. (92, 93) With the availability of good chemical dyes and commercially dyed threads, the colors used on the pants stayed brighter and did not run. Mien women in refugee camps had time to embroider almost all day, sitting and talking with other women, sharing designs, comparing embroidery, and trying new colors. Not only did they have time to make themselves more clothes than ever before, but the clothes lasted longer because they were no longer doing farm work, and much of the time the younger women wore sarongs instead of their traditional Mien pants. (96)

Younger women in particular no longer wanted to be seen in their old style, sparsely embroidered pants. They wanted new pants solidly covered with brightly colored cross-stitch designs. They wanted fabric with a finer weave so they could get more designs on their pants. The emphasis was no longer on making utilitarian every day work pants, but on making super beautiful, special occasion works of art that would show all their skill and industriousness and all the new designs.

Yien Sio, Muey Sio's younger sister remembers, "In camp in 1978 I did one pair of pants all cross-stitch. Lots of free time in camp. I saw people use more beautiful designs and fill in more. I learned *zangh-piaeng* (steamer) and rhinocerous tail. I used them on my pants because I just wanted to keep them like a sampler." (97)

zangh-piaeng
rice steamer

sux gorc dueiv, baeqc miuh caengx
rhinocerous tail, Hmong umbrella

In the late 1970s and '80s as people began to leave the camps for their third country of resettlement, often the United States, they had to make some difficult choices.

Muey Sio recalls, "In 1979 when we finished the interviews to come to this country, I had to decide what to take. They said each person could take twenty kilos. We didn't have a scale, and we didn't know what they would let us take and what they wouldn't let us take. We left lots of things like baskets and clothes. Some of the clothes we left were still good. We gave

34

92. Sampler with numerous Thai Mien designs. Designs such as these were copied by Mien refugees in Chiang Kham Camp and sold for much-needed cash. Lois Callaway collection. SC

93. Zangx-piaeng or rice steamer design sampler. The bottom design was done using "new" blue thread in place of the more traditional white thread used in the top design. Lois Callaway collection. SC

94. A pants' panel made for Lois Callaway using nontraditional colors. Lois Callaway collection. SC

95. Comparison of pants made in Chiang Kham Camp in the late 1970s (left, Tsan On Saelee) with pants prefered by American Mien in the 1990s (right, Muey Sio Fong). Colors have changed and design elements have been fragmented and recombined. AG

96. *Chiang Kham Refugee Camp, Thailand, 1990. Young women prefered Thai sarongs to traditional Mien clothes, which made them more conspicuous. LD*

97. *Pants made by Yien Sio Saechao in Chiang Kham Refugee Camp, 1978. Visible are rhinocerous tail or Hmong design, comb of the faam-cing bird, big blossom, rice steamer, dragon, and tiger ears designs among others. San Jose, California. SC*

98. *Examining an old embroidered wedding square that the owner wished to sell. Chiang Kham Refugee Camp, 1990. LD*

99. *A Mien family in Chiang Kham Refugee Camp being photographed in preparation for emigration, probably to the United States. 1990. LD*

100. Women in a northern Thai village listening to a taped message from American relatives. Woman on left has her turban wrapped Thai style, and woman on right has diagonally wrapped northern Lao style turban. 1990. AG

101. Mien woman with baby shopping for embroidery thread, Berkeley, California, 1992. AG

102. Women in northern Thailand embroidering pants to sell to American relatives. Woman on right wears pants typical of Nan Province, woman in center wears red pants of Chiangrai Province, and woman on left is wearing a sarong. All work on finely woven fabric with the specific blue and yellow colored threads demanded by fashion-conscious Western Mien. 1990. LD

103. *Old style northern Lao pants with widely spaced, mostly white designs compared to Muey Sio Fong's intricately embroidered colorful pants which are typical of the pants prefered by all Western Mien. AG*

104. *French Mien also order pants made in Thailand with the same specifications demanded by their American cousins. Photo by Mey Meng Saeteun, daughter of Ying Kwen, on a trip to France to visit relatives in 1993.*

105. *Family in Oakland, California with newly embroidered pants made in the United States and heirloom pieces brought from Laos. 1991. AG*

106. Pet Fong Saelee's new coat with old style loose ruff made from maroon silk yarn. Richmond, California. SC

107. Pet Fong Saelee holding the three pairs of pants she is saving for her funeral. 1991. Richmond, California. SC

108. New pants made in California by Fuay Lium with new colors on finely woven fabric but using all old designs in weave- and grid-stitches. AG

109. Scrap from Mien pants found by Jane Hanks on a road in northern Thailand in the 1960s. AG

110. Six pairs of Mien pants showing the increasing amounts of blue and bright yellow used from about 1950 to the 1990s. AG

111. Pants made by Liw Sieng Saeteun in 1966 in Nam Kueng, Laos, when she was eighteen years old (right), and a new pair ordered from Thailand in the 1990s (left). Oakland, California. AG

112. Young Mien women in turbans in a northern Thai village. 1988. AG

those to relatives. Old things, not so good, I left there. I threw in the big hole they dig for the garbage. After we left, my mother-in-law said many other people came to collect those old things. Many people sell those old things, so now they don't have to throw away. (98, 99)

"In the camp, I wore Mien clothes. After I interviewed, I tried to wear Thai clothes a little bit. I didn't know some people would wear Mien clothes to come here. If I knew, I would have worn my Mien clothes. When we flew, I saw Meuy Yoon and her mother-in-law dressed in Mien, and I saw her and her husband walk around, look outside, say this and say that. But I didn't know her then. I was very scared, and I didn't walk around.

"Some people came to the United States before, and they sent cassettes. I remember they said we didn't have to take our old clothes. We wouldn't be able to use them. And it's true. We brought lots of clothes, and some we don't use. We wear different clothes here." (100)

LIFE IN THE UNITED STATES

When they left Thailand to settle in the United States, many people took embroidery supplies with them. Eventually, they found acceptable sources for fabric and threads in the United States, but their relatives still in Thailand also sent them supplies. (101)

People continued to embroider as they adjusted to their new country. But as they got jobs and enrolled in classes they wore their Mien clothes less often and valued their time more. They were also eager to help the relatives still in Thailand.

By the mid 1980s many Mien women in the United States were buying pants sent from Thailand instead of making their own. A rather large industry in clothes for American Mien developed in the refugee camps and in the Mien villages. Mien women in Thai villages wear the colors of their area but embroider pants for sale in colors preferred by the Western Mien. (102)

Fey Chien in Richmond, California says, "Before, I was very poor. Now I make some money, and I bought these things from Thailand. If I work two, three days here, I can get them, but in Thailand I sew every day for one-half year."

Yien Sio, who lives in San Jose, had started a new pair of pants for herself in 1987, but because she works she had no time to finish them. She sent fabric and thread to her sister still in Thailand, and paid her to finish them. She says she bought about 144 skeins of floss for these pants. Good fine weave, cotton fabric can cost $20 a yard, so the outlay for materials alone was probably more than $100. The embroidery takes hundreds of hours.

Even though seldom worn in the United States, the traditional clothing is still considered essential. The clothes are an integral part of Mien marriage arrangements and of the ceremony itself, and women plan ahead for their children's and grandchildren's weddings. Not only bride and groom and their attendants but most female guests in the bride's extended family and many on the groom's side as well are expected to display their most recently acquired Mien clothing and silver. These outfits represent an enormous investment in time and money. (50)

In the mid 1980s new pants from Thailand cost around $200, and by 1992 they cost close to $400, more than some Thai villagers earn in a year. Pants and other garments are sent to relatives in the United States who show them around, sell them, and send the money back to Thailand. Of course, if the colors aren't right or the weave of the fabric too coarse, no one will pay the high price. Competition has resulted in a strict standardization of colors and in finer and finer embroidery.

Fashionable Western Mien, no matter which area of Laos or Thailand they originally came from, want pants made of extremely fine cotton even-weave fabric which makes the embroidery stitches minute and very time consuming and hard to do. A far greater number of colors is used than on the pants of a generation ago. (103) Except for the traditional weave- and grid-stitch rows on the bottom section of the pants which remain almost the same, the entire two panels are solidly cross-stitched in a rich variety of patterns and colors. The colors of choice are deep yellow, bright ice blue, dark maroon or brown, and deep royal blue. Smaller amounts of other colors are used according to individual taste, but the primary colors are very specific, and Mien women all over California, Oregon, Washington, Canada, and France use the same color numbers from the same embroidery thread company for at least three of these colors. (104) They now search internationally for the perfect thread, the perfect color. Red wool yarn for coat ruffs comes from England and France, silk from Hong Kong and Thailand, embroidery and tassel threads from the United States, Germany, Laos, and China. But they also joke about how many supplies they have tucked away in closets that they will probably never use.

Yet, most young American Mien girls are clearly not learning to embroider. As their mothers say, they must go to school here and learn to read. They have no time to embroider. And the mothers, too, are busy. They work or go to school to learn English and have no time or patience to teach their daughters. It's too hard to teach them, they say, and they will only "wear Mien" once, probably, for their wedding. It's much easier to buy the garments from Thailand.

Seng Van, born in Laos in 1970, had a big Mien wedding in Oakland, California in 1985 and when interviewed was in a computer training program. She says, "You buy from Thailand, new. In Thailand embroidery is one way to make a living. I don't know how to do this (embroidery). I can do these small x's (cross-stitch), but I can't do any of these (weave- and grid-stitches). I did a little bit, but I threw them away. I can't even put on a turban for an hour. It hurts my head. After five or ten minutes my head starts itching. My children won't wear Mien at their wedding. They prefer American clothes. It's not important to have things from your culture. It's a waste of money and takes too much time."

There are still a few older women who continue to embroider traditional clothing and who have enviable collections of heirloom pieces brought with them from Laos. (105) Others make new Western style garments or accessories they can use here such as hand bags, skirts and men's ties using Mien embroidery designs. But even women who are no longer doing much embroidery still think they might in the future. They still examine new pants from Thailand and copy new designs onto their sample cloths. And they continue to buy embroidery supplies when they find colors or fabrics that appeal to them.

Older women who are concerned about their own welfare in the after-life worry about the change in tradition. Maybe the new designs are not acceptable in the spirit world. Meuy Yoon says, "When they're buried, they have to have clothes. Old people say when you die you have to take all the cross-stitching out because the ancestors already in the spirit world don't use. Cross-stitch cannot go through the heaven. You go half way to the other side, and they say to go away. Also can't use wool. Need silk."

Many women are saving some older more traditional pants for their own burial. Pet Fong, now in her eighties, has saved three pairs of pants representing three distinct styles: one with cross-stitching, one old with no cross-stitching and one intermediate style. (107) She also has a new coat with a maroon silk ruff, unlike the modern red wool ruffs. This color matches a tasseled silver ornament she made when she was fourteen. The coat fabric is hand-spun, hand-woven cotton, not the modern polished cotton. (106) Some older women are making new pants with the finer weave fabric and the fashionable new colors but using the old designs, the old style. (108)

Few people see any need to save old clothing that is out of style. For the few special occasions when they "dress Mien" they want to wear stylish new clothes, and they are convinced that their children will always be uninterested in past styles. When there are opportunities to market their embroidery, many women cut up their out of style traditional clothing to make shoulder bags and coin purses for sale to westerners. (68)

CONCLUSIONS

LOOKING FOR CLUES

Jane Hanks, while in Thailand with her husband doing anthropological field work in the 1960s, picked up a scrap of embroidered fabric on the road. It is the bottom few inches of a pair of Mien pants and is very tattered. She recently gave this scrap to the author who showed it to six Mien women and recorded their comments. (109)

All agreed that the fabric was very fine and was probably woven by Lantien or *canh zeiv* people and that it was also well-dyed because "it's still black, not blue". And they agreed it was made by someone from Laos because of the kind of weave-stitch, *Wuanh Guangv*, used on the almost non-existent bottom row and because of the amount of white in the designs. Some said the white had originally been dipped in an indigo bath but the indigo had all worn off.

The embroidery thread was of several kinds. The fine white thread they called *sa'laqv suix* which they translated as communist or soldier thread saying it came from Vietnam. The coarser white thread was probably *canh zeiv* like the fabric. The red, green, and some of the black threads were commercial pearl cotton.

About the embroidery itself, they were all somewhat critical. They immediately found lots of mistakes which were at first attributed to the sloppiness of the embroiderer. But since most of the embroidery was extremely fine work, they soon added more thoughtful explanations. Muey Sio said, "The *som* here, look at this color! Some filled in and some not. Maybe it's the first time she tried this. Sometimes mothers just let daughters try something on their pants. On the end it's very sloppy but the other part's very fine." Muey Yoon said, "When you first learn, you just start. Try (embroidering) on your mother's pants, or find old piece like this and practice on it." Ying Kwen added, "In Laos they're very poor. They wear patch where there are too many holes. You save to patch something." And she recalled, "For us we had one aunt, and we always gave old pants to her. She could talk, but she had difficulty learning. She could make straight lines and patching."

Frayed and worn though it is, because of the presence of pearl cotton and because of the fineness of the cloth and the closeness of the *som* pattern, the women thought the piece could not have been done much before the mid-1960s.

On the other hand, some of the oldest existing examples of Mien pants and pants' panels have never been worn and are in beautiful condition. These are often the last or best pants made by someone's grandmother or great-grandmother and were carried out of Laos, carefully wrapped, as family heirlooms. Some are said to be as old as eighty to a hundred years. It is hard to distinguish these from pants made forty or fifty years later since the fashions and available supplies do not seem to have changed much during that time.

As people moved out of their villages and into refugee centers such as Nam Thouei and Nam Kueng the younger girls and women began to be enamored with the new designs and stitches seen there, but their mothers and aunts still resisted change. Thus pants made in the late fifties and early sixties can be very "old fashioned" with widely spaced designs done in weave- and grid-stitch with few colors, or they can have more closely spaced designs, more colors and some rows of cross-stitching. The particularly lovely style of pants with rows of colorful cross-stitched designs alternating with rows of white grid-stitch *som* designs, "A number One" pants, developed during the late 1960s and early 1970s. During this time women also began to dip white threads in the indigo bath or run them through bluing powder giving them a light blue tint which generally wore off after a short while. (110)

Almost all Mien pants made since 1975 have ever-increasing amounts of cross-stitching on them and more and darker blue threads replacing white. Since the 1980s colors tend to have changed from lighter blues, yellows, magentas, greens, and reds to the very deep blue, dark yellow, maroon/brown and green preferred in the 1990s. And the more recent pants are done on extremely fine, often commercially woven, cotton fabric. New designs are often parts of older designs, segmented and rearranged into more intricate patterns. These new patterns are often unnammed. (24, 95)

Liew Sieng who is in her forties and lives in Oakland, California has six pairs of pants. Two she brought with her from Thailand. One is the old style which her mother made for her in Laos. It has spaced designs, no cross-stitch, lots of white embroidery. One she made for herself in Laos in the 1970s using rows of cross-stitch alternating with rows of traditional *som* design. White threads were probably given a brief dyeing in indigo.

When she came to California in 1979 she brought threads with her and made a pair solidly covered with cross-stitch similar to what she saw people doing in the refugee camp. Instead of white she used a blue thread she dyed with commercial colorfast dye. She still calls this color white because it replaces what was traditionally white. But the three most recent pants were made by someone in Thailand in the mid-1980s who sent them to California to sell. These are all on fine fabric, and the dominant colors are bright blue and yellow. Most of the traditional designs have been replaced by newly created cross-stitch designs. She doesn't know the names of many of them. And she never wears any of these pants, but she says, "I need a lot. My children might get married. For their wives." (111)

CHANGES IN THAILAND AND LAOS

When I visited Mien villages in northern Thailand in January, 1988, almost all the women were wearing at least something traditionally Mien. Some of the younger women were only wearing the turban, (112), but the older women were wearing the complete Mien outfit. (1) Most men under forty were wearing T-shirts or cotton indigo shirts and baggy pants, typical of most Thai farmers. But many older men wore berets, and some wore traditional Mien jackets, sash, and pants.

On subsequent visits, only a few young women were wearing anything to distinguish them as Mien. Most other women were in simple blouses and sarongs and were indistinguishable from the local Thai women. In 1992 villages looked more prosperous, less distinctly Mien. Electricity was available in every household, televisions were visible in many homes, and some women had become successful entrepreneurs managing the assembling, buying, and selling of traditional Mien clothing destined for their comparatively wealthy relatives in North America and France.

Other villages more remote do not have the same opportunities for communication and trade with the outside world, but almost all are becoming more aware of progress and opportunities. Almost all have some relative in the United States with whom they can communicate by means of cassettes and battery-run tape recorders. Women in all these villages continue to embroider for their own needs and, if they have the time and the connections, for outsiders, at a price. They are also being approached by Thais and others wishing to buy old clothes. This new source of easy cash has persuaded many to part with all but their newest, most fashionable clothes.

Most Mien in the United States have a strong desire to return to Thailand, Laos, and China to visit relatives, and many have already done so, some several times. They take with them gifts of cash, clothes, and embroidery supplies. As Meuy Yoon Phan says, "Those people (the Chinese Mien) can use. They wear clothes, the colors are different, but now maybe they want to use some kind of color their sister or brother here tell them about."

They bring back video cassettes recording everything they see and hear on their journeys. Upon their return these cassettes are eagerly viewed by all their relatives and friends.

Toud Kuei Law, who has not yet returned to visit, says, "I think the young people (in Laos) wear Lao clothes, but the older ones wear Mien clothes. When I go back there, I won't wear Mien clothes. I'll wear Laos clothes or American clothes. Now we already take off our hat (turban). Before, in our country we never take off our hat, nobody sees our hair. Now we don't like it, too heavy. I think the young people they wear like us. They have a hard time to embroider, they're working hard. My sister in Laos, raises pigs. It's all raining, dirty, all mud. When I saw that I almost cried because when they eat, there's no light, nothing, very dark. I'm very sorry for them.

"So many people here go visit there, they bought a lot of clothes to give people there. In the video movie they have from Laos, they always wear American clothes with name on it, the brand. Man and woman. No Smoking, Adidas, something on the T-shirt. If I go back to Laos, I have to take the floss for embroidery because over there they cannot find enough floss for embroidery. That's why they have to buy Thai or Lao clothes to wear. In the video some have the turban on, but on the body put the Lao clothes."

THOUGHTS ON THE FUTURE

Muey Sio and her mother, Liw Chian, Liw Sieng, Meuy Yoon, Muey Seng, Ying Kwen, Toud Kuei, and all the other women interviewed have spent the last thirty years struggling to hold their families and traditions together. Brothers, sisters, parents, husbands, and many, many children have been lost to war and sickness. They have undergone hardships and worked incredibly hard to provide their families with the necessities of life.

But now in the United States it does not seem possible for their children to comprehend what a high price was paid for what is viewed as a better life. The children are tired of hearing about how difficult life was in Laos, and many parents have stopped trying to tell them of their experiences.

Toud Kouei's daughter, a high school honor student when interviewed, said that she's not interested in Mien things, she doesn't believe what her parents tell her. At the same time she says she wants to learn more about the Mien because her teachers ask her, but she wants to read it in books. Unfortunately, there is very little written about the Mien for her to read, and most people of her parents' generation have had little or no schooling and cannot read or write.

Although most Western Mien, with reliable sources of income, medical care, education, food, and housing feel they are much better off than their relatives in Southeast Asia, they are not always convinced they have done the right thing by leaving. They face problems here, too. Children appear to be unconcerned about carrying on the traditions, they are forgetting the customs, forgetting Mien, the girls don't learn embroidery, and the boys will probably never learn to conduct the religious ceremonies necessary to care for their elders after they die. Many people are converting to Christianity, and some are marrying non-Mien.

The older people begin to view these changes as inevitable. But they continue to show their own cultural loyalty by doing the religious ceremonies in the best way possible, by spending more time and money on the preparations, the priests, the food, and the clothing, thus doing their utmost to imprint Mien-ness on their children and to provide for the welfare of their ancestors. But even though religious observances seem to be flourishing, the purchase of new traditional Mien clothing is dwindling. By the spring of 1994 the price of new Mien pants from Thailand was beginning to drop, and American Mien were telling their Thai relatives not to send more. Everyone already has a supply of a lifetime, and there are no more refugees arriving from Thailand. Most Mien children who are now growing up in the United States will probably not feel compelled to make or buy expensive Mien clothes for their own children.

Muey Sio, talking about the changes, says, "Some older people worry here about the spirits and the religious ceremonies. Nobody will know how to do it unless the young children learn how. First they have to learn to read and write Chinese, and then they can learn to do the ceremonies. Now there aren't so many who know how to teach. They have to have a teacher who studied a lot and learned all the books. The one they have now studied high. He has twenty to thirty students, but they're small still, and when they're older, they'll have no time or they won't be interested.

"I don't see anybody now who is learning the embroidery. If we're gone, they probably won't know how to do it anymore. The older people worry, but they can't do anything about it. The young people don't know how to dress, how to put the turban on. They don't want to use those kinds of clothes.

"Now the parents make or buy for them. When they get married, probably that's the only time they will wear Mien clothes. I don't know what they'll do with the clothes. Just put in the closet. But they'll always be Mien."

Teen-aged Mien girl in her holiday finery. Northern Thailand 1950s. Photo by Sylvia Lombard.

GLOSSARY OF MIEN WORDS

The tone of each written Mien word is indicated by the letter or lack of letter at the end of the word. Simplified, *x* indicates a rising tone, *v* is a high tone, *h* is a falling tone, *z* rises and then falls, *c* is a low tone, and no final consonant indicates a middle tone. *Q* when it appears at the end of a word indicates a short, cut-off ending, a glottal stop. *Sieqv*, the word for girl, is pronounced like "see a" but with a high tone and a short, cut-off ending.

Some of the letters within the words themselves have pronunciations unlike English. The letter *c* is pronounced like an English *ts*. *Q* at the beginning of a word is like an English aspirated *ch* as in the initial *ch* in *church*. *J* is like an unaspirated *ch* as in the final *ch* of *church*. *Nq* is pronounced like a *g*, and *nj* is pronounced like a *j*. Thus, the word *nqimh*, pinchers, is pronounced "ghim" with a falling tone, and the word for embroidery, *congx*, is pronounced "tsong" with a rising tone as if there were a question mark after it. *Or* is pronounced like English *aw*, so the word for spider, *ga'nyorc*, is pronounced "ganyaw." More or less.

M or *n* preceding some consonants at the beginning of a word are not pronounced but indicate that the consonant is voiced rather than unvoiced.

To an English speaker, many of the sounds are indistinguishable. *Buoz*, arm or hand, *buo*, three, *mbuo*, group or plural indicator, *mbuoqc*, bag or pocket, *mbuox*, name, and *mbuov*, blue, sound very similar to someone unfamiliar with tonal languages and voiced, unvoiced, aspirated and unaspirated sounds.

Even though there is now, since 1984, a unified system for the spelling of Mien words, there has as yet been no definitive Mien dictionary published using Roman script. Therefore, since Mien from different regions often pronounce words quite differently, it can sometimes be difficult to decide on a proper spelling.

It should be noted that the romanized spelling of Mien names does not usually follow the above rules. For most refugees, the official spelling of their name was determined by western authorities interviewing them in Thailand. There was little uniformity in the spelling since different officials heard and thus spelled the names differently. The *Sae* prefix on last names was used by the Thai and Lao governments to indicate Chinese clan names. At one time this was used for all people of Chinese decent. Many Mien drop this prefix when they become United States citizens, as they themselves do not use it.

ba'finx - An elaborate piece of jewelry worn on the back of a woman's coat. It can have Chinese glass beads, silver chains, tassels, enameled fish and flowers, and amulets in the shape of pestles, fish, sesame seeds, scissors, tweezers, and the like.

baaih - A fringe.

baeqc - White. Can mean blue when used to refer to the blue colored thread that has replaced the traditional white color of certain embroidery designs on modern Mien pants.

baeqc miuh - Hmong. White Hmong.

baeqc miuh biangh - Hmong flower. A cross-stitch design.

benx - To embellish, enrich, or add to. Often applied to cross-stitch designs that have been rearranged or modified in some way.

beu - To wrap up.

biangh - Flower, blossom. An embroidery design done in cross-stitch. Also the term used for appliqué design motifs.

biauv - House, home.

biei - Hair.

binh zangv - A diagonal hemming stitch.

buih dorh - Refers to the weight of a balance scale. A cross-stitch design.

buih dorh benx - An elaborated or enriched *buih dorh* design.

buix - To carry something over the shoulder or slung from the shoulder.

buonv- An example.

buoz - Arm.

buoz-jiemh - Bracelet.

buoz-zamh - The length of outstretched arms. A length of measure.

buoz-zaux camv - Many hands and feet. A weave-, grid-, or cross-stitch design.

canh zei - Lantien people.

caengx - To support, prop up.

camv - Much, many.

ceix - Sharp.

cing-jiouc dueiv - Tail of the *cing-jiouc* bird. A small version of the weave-stitch design called *ga'nyorc*.

congx - Embroidery.

congx-benx - Embroidery designs that have been embellished, added to, or rearranged but have not been given any particular name.

congx-beu - Embroidery wrapper. A square of cloth, hemmed and decorated with embroidery used for wrapping up embroidery work-in-progress and supplies to keep them clean.

congx-buonv - Sample cloth. A scrap of fabric used to record new designs or parts of designs.

congx-caengx - Supporting embroidery. A grid-stitch design with a central row or cross of stitches from which radiate smaller designs.

congx-ceix - Spiked or sharp embroidery. A weave-stitch embroidery design.

congx congx - To do embroidery.

congx-dorn - Small, narrow section of weave-stitch embroidery near the bottom of a pant leg.

congx-ga'nyorc - Spider embroidery. The section of a woman's embroidered pants that traditionally had spider designs on it.

congx-gapv - Puzzle or box design. A cross-stitch design. Can also refer to a design created by fitting together several repeats of a smaller design element to form a new design.

congx-jiemc - Weave-stitch embroidery. *Jiemc* means to go in and out with the needle doing several stitches at a time.

congx-mbiaatc - A weave-stitch embroidery design used on the bottom border of women's pants. *Mbiaatc* refers to a fan used by priests in religious rituals.

congx-niouv - Twisted embroidery. An embroidery design done in weave- or grid-stitch.

congx-nyietv - Cross-stitch embroidery. *Nyietv* means to tie up.

congx-nzaangc - An old weave-stitch design. *Nzaangc* means Chinese characters.

congx-setv - The top edge, finishing, or end row of the weave-stitch embroidery section at the bottom of a pant leg.

congx-sieqv - Little girl embroidery. Design done in weave-stitch. This is often the first design young girls learn to do. When done in grid-stitch it is called *som*.

congx-tiu - Grid-stitch embroidery. *Tiu* means to pick or hook something up. Similar to Holbein stitch in western embroidery books.

cunx - To string or thread. *Cunx zou,* to string beads.

cuoh muoqc - A tree of which the wood or roots are used to make maroon dye with.

da'jungh ndiangx - *Da'jungh* tree. The tree used to construct the bridge for bridge ceremonies connecting this world with the world of the gods. Also used to make *guaax dang* stools and tubs for holding dye baths or water. A weave-stitch design.

daai - To hang down.

deih - Hoof or foot.

domh - Big, important, older. Can also mean middle.

domh biangh dueiv - Big blossom tail. A cross-stitch design.

domh congx - Big, wide section of weave-stitch embroidery near the bottom of a woman's pants leg.

domh jauv congx - Middle of the road embroidery. The embroidery placed in the central section of a woman's turban.

domh jienv jiemc - Big gibbon design done in weave-stitch.

domh paax - A large indigo-dyed and embroidered cloth used as the main covering of the bride's wedding hat.

don - Stool.

dongh zinh - Copper Chinese coins with holes in the middle. Used as weights on bobbins for making braided cording.

dongh zinh ngau - A small section of bamboo with a short stem left on as a hook. Used as a bobbin for making braided cording.

dorn - Son. Small.

dueiv - Tail.

dungz - Pig.

dungz-dorn deih - Baby pig's hoof. An old weave-stitch design.

dunh - Silk material.

dun-junh - A many-paneled silk skirt, also called *la'mienv junh* worn by initiates and by priests during religious ceremonies.

fam - To add to or to fill in. One can fill in spaces in a row of seedlings where not all seeds have germinated, or one can add more designs to fill empty spaces between designs on an embroidered cloth.

Faam-Cing - The Three Pure Ones. The three Taoist gods ruling over the highest heaven who appear in several of the religious paintings used by the Mien in ceremonies. Also the name of a bird.

faam-cing nqun - The comb of the *faam-cing* bird. A cross-stitch design.

faam-cing dueiv - The tail of the *faam-cing* design. Part of the larger design.

fei - Silk, thread. Embroidery thread, both silk and cotton is usually referred to as *fei*.

fei-baeqc - White thread. A particular color of blue thread now used for designs that were traditionally white is also called *fei baeqc*, especially by older women.

fim - The central part, heart, or sprout of such plants as palm, bamboo, banana, and ginger.

finx - Thin strands or wires.

ga'maeqc - Corn, maize.

ga'maeqc mbeux or *maeqc mbeux* - Popcorn. A design done in weave-, grid-, or cross-stitch.

ga'nyorc - Spider. The name of an embroidery design done in grid- or weave-stitch. Also the name of the section of embroidery on women's pants where the grid- or weave-stitch spider designs were traditionally done.

ga'nyorc-benx - Enriched spider design. Spider designs that have been altered from the traditional one. Weave- or grid-stitch.

ga'nyorc-jieqv - Black spider. Groupings in the spider section with black design elements are called *ga'nyorh jieqv*. Weave- or grid-stitch.

ga'nyorc-joih - An arrangement or grouping of designs in the spider section of a woman's embroidered pants.

ga'nyorc-nquaav - Chipped or unfinished spider design. This small design done in grid- or weave-stitch is in the shape of a square with a triangular section left out of one side. It is done in the *ga'nyorh* section of the pants.

gaeng - Insect or bug. Also the name of a stitch similar to the buttonhole stitch used with braid as a decorative couching stitch, on tassels, and as netting on good luck charms and ornaments.

gaam-zaiv-neix - Stem of an orange. Another name for the small *maeqc mbeux* design.

gapv - To fit together like a puzzle. A box with a lid.

gitv - To braid. *Gitv hlaang* is to weave braided cording with the fingers.

gomv - To cover.

guh nguaaz - Baby or child.

guh nguaaz muoc - Baby hat.

guh nguaaz zaanh doic - Baby bib.

guaan - Yarn of wool, synthetic, cotton, or silk, used as pompoms or ruffs.

guaax dang - An important merit-making ceremony.

guaax dang don - A special stool for the *guaax daangv* ceremony. The name of a cross-stitch design.

heh - Shoes.

heh tongv - Boots. Now rare. They are made of heavy, white cotton fabric and decorated with red applique, finger braid, and tassels.

hiun - Earring, as in *m'normh hiun,* the traditional Mien earring in the form of an incomplete circle.

hlaang - Braided cording. Woven on the fingers with loops of thread or done with bobbins on a frame. Used as an edging on many garments and accessories.

hlaang-mbiorngz - An ornament worn hanging down from the back of the neck of a woman's coat. It consists of long strands of braid wrapped with silver wire and with tassels or silver bells on the ends.

hlaengx - A section of something. A triangular cross-stitch design.

hlopv - To tighten with a drawstring.

hnaangx-zaang-yangh biangh - Flower for coloring steamed rice yellow. Also used for dyeing threads. The purple flower from the butterfly bush.

hongh - Bright red.

hongc mbiorngz - A red cloth which is part of the wedding hat covering the bride's head.

houx - Pants.

houx-caamv - The extra piece of cloth or gusset added to the bottom edge of a pant leg to make it wider.

houx-nqenx - Embroidered pants with narrow alternating rows of cross-stitch and grid-stitch.

houx-sin - The body or upper part of the pants. The part above the *houx-zauz*.

houx-zaux - The leg of the embroidered pants. The bottom part with the traditional weave- and grid-stitch designs.

huaa - Flower (literary language).

hungh - King.

jaang - Neck.

jaang-waanh - Necklace made of solid silver.

jangc - Boy, man.

jangc dorn - Male.

jangc dorn hlaang - Man's waist sash.

jangc dorn houx - Man's pants.

jangc dorn lui - Man's jacket.

jangc m'nqorngv beu - Man's turban.

janx - Outsider, non-Mien.

janx-dorn - Child. Non-Mien.

janx-dorn ngamv - A child squatting. A cross-stitch design.

janx-gekv - Lowland Northern Thai or Lao who are often the village merchants and are thus considered rich. They tend to build their houses on the ground, not up on poles. Some say they are Chinese (Cantonese).

janx-gekv tei - Stairs of *janx gekv* people. A cross-stitch design.

janx-taiv - Thai people.

janx-taiv biauv - Thai houses. A cross-stitch design.

jauv - Road.

jiemc - Going in and out with a needle taking several stitches at a time.

jienv - Gibbon. An embroidery design done in weave- or grid-stitch.

jienv-jiemc - Gibbon design done in weave-stitch.

jienv-tiu - Gibbon design done in grid-stitch.

jienv-dorn - Small gibbon design.

jienv-ngau - Crooked gibbon design.

jienv-saa - Spaced gibbon. A design with many evenly spaced or separated legs.

jieqv - Black.

jiex - To sew, as in *jiex hlaang,* to sew braid on the edge of something like a purse or ornament.

joih - Bunch, as in a bunch of grapes.

jorngx - To hang from the shoulder.

jorngx-guaan - Yarn pompoms on a shoulder bag.

jouv coix - Chive.

jouv coix biangh - Chive flower. A cross-stitch design.

jung - Dragon.

jung-hinc - Rainbow. One of the forms the dragon can take. A cross-stitch design.

jung hungh - Dragon king who lives in the water. A cross-stitch design. Also written *ju'hungh* in its contracted form.

junh - Round. Something that wraps around.

kuangx - To hang, as in *kuangx ziem,* to hang (do) the *ziem* stitch.

la'kaux - Button.

la'kaux-mbeih - Flat button. Big, rectangular, silver buttons or buckles used on the front opening of women's coats.

la'kaux-junh - Round silver buttons used on men's jackets.

la'kaux-kuotv - Button hole made from looped braid.

la'baeng - Leggings.

la'baeng-baeqc - White embroidered leggings worn by women during very important ceremonies. Seldom worn anymore.

la'mienv junh - A many-paneled skirt, also called *dunh junh,* worn by priests during religious ceremonies.

la'sin - Woman's embroidered sash made of indigo-dyed cotton cloth. Everyday sash.

la'sin-baeqc - White embroidered sash made of narrow unbleached cotton cloth. Special ceremonial sash.

la'sin-congx - Embroidered sash made of indigo-dyed cotton cloth. Different from *la'sin* because it is embroidered with older designs covering a large part of the sash, and it has tassels on the ends. Special ceremonial sash.

limc - Chain.

lomh zeuv - Old embroidery design done in grid-stitch. Women insist these words apply only to this design and to nothing else.

louc - To twist or twine like a vine

Luh Guon - A spirit.

Luh Guon-fim - A cross-stitch design. *Fim,* as in *Luh Guon fim,* refers to the central growing part of such plants as palm, bamboo, banana, and ginger.

Luh Guon yienx - *Luh Guon's* stamp. An old cross-stitch design.

Luh Guon louc - Twining or trailing *Luh Guon* design. Done in cross-stitch in a row and traditionally used on the neck facing of a woman's coat.

lui - Jacket, coat.

lui-gaeng - A man's padded vest with Chinese coin buttons down the front.

lui-guaax - A long ritual tunic worn by priests during religious ceremonies.

lui-guaan - The yarn ruff on the neck of the woman's coat.

lui-jaang-nqom- Woman's coat neck covering. A small mid-section of the *lui-laengh* at the back of the neck made with white cloth. Usually embroidered.

lui-laengh - Embroidered neck facing on a woman's coat. Made with even-weave indigo-dyed fabric except for a small white section at the back of the neck.

lui-leiz - Narrow strips of colored cotton fabric appliqued as edgings on some garments.

lunh - To sew using a simple running stitch. Used for sewing two pieces of fabric together.

m'normh - Ear.

m'normh hiun - Earring.

m'nqorngv - Head.

m'nqorngv-beu - Turban.

m'nqorngv-mbiorngz - A piece of cloth used to cover the head as a sun shade.

m'nqorngv-limc - Long chains of silver which are wrapped diagonally around the woman's turban.

m'zuv huaa - *M'zuv* flower. *M'zuv* is believed to be a Chinese name of a flower. An old cross-stitch design.

maaz-geqc - Stilts.

maeng - Green.

maeqc mbeux - Popcorn. Also *ga'maeqc mbeux.*

maaqc - Touching, crowded together.

mba'biei - Human hair.

mba'biei-muoc - A stiff, black hat made from woven human hair worn by a priest while conducting ceremonies.

mba'hinx - A small black bird, probably a swallow or swift, that often builds its nest in the house thatch and "talks" to the household. Some women claim this bird brings good luck.

mba'hinx dueiv - Tail of the *mba'hinx* bird. A small version of the weave-stitch design called *ga'nyorh.*

mba'hnoi - Sun.

mba'hnoi biangh - Sunflower. A cross-stitch design.

mba'ong - Thunder, a powerful force.

mba'ong-don - Thunder's stool. A weave-stitch design.

mbaih - Row or line.

mbatc - Hook shape.

mbeux - Explode.

mbiaapc - A fan used by priests in religious rituals.

mbiauz - Fish.

mbiauz-mbungv - Fish bones. An old weave-stitch design.

mbiorngz - To cover.

mbungv - Bone.

mbuoqc - Bag or pocket.

mbuoqc hlopv - A small cloth bag, sometimes embroidered, closed at the top with drawstrings.

mbuoqc jorngx - Large shoulder bag made from hand-loomed striped fabric, one long piece forming the shoulder strap with a shorter piece forming the central body of the bag. It is decorated with elongated pompoms and appliqué designs.

mbuov - Blue.

muoc - Hat.

muoc-guaan - Yarn pompoms on baby hats.

muoqc - Tree (literary language).

naetv - To sew using a whip stitch. Used when sewing two braided cords together or for sewing flat braid around the edges of appliquéd pieces, *naetv biaangh*.

nda'maauh - Tiger, considered powerful and beautiful. Many of the tiger designs have interchangeable names. All are done in cross-stitch.

nda'maauh biorngh - Tiger's forehead. A cross-stitch design.

nda'maauh ndopv - Tiger's skin. A cross-stitch design.

nda'maauh m'normh- Tiger's ears. A cross-stitch design.

nda'maauh m'normh gapv - Tiger's ears design pieced together to form a larger compound design. A cross-stitch design.

nda'maauh nyiuv - Tiger's claws. A cross-stitch design.

ndaan - An open storage basket.

ndaauv - Long.

ndatv - The verb used with the *gaeng* stitch. *Ndatv gaeng,* to do the buttonhole stitch.

ndiangx - Tree.

ndie-maeng - Dark blue-black, indigo-dyed cloth. *Maeng* actually means green refering to the color of the indigo dye bath.

ndie-baeqc - Handspun, handwoven, even-weave cotton fabric produced by various peoples of Thailand, Laos, and Burma such as the Tai Leu, Tai Dam, Lantien, Shan, or Akha who grow, spin, and weave cotton.

ndie-jieqv - Black-dyed cloth. Cloth dyed with indigo. It is then over-dyed with other plant dyes to make it almost black.

ndioux - As in *ndioux hlaang,* to make braided cording using bobbins.

ndopv - Skin.

ngamv - To squat.

ngau - Crooked.

nienv - To roll a hem as in *nienv binh zangv,* to sew a rolled hem with *binh zangv* stitch.

niouv - Twisted.

njaamh - Indigo.

njimh - Pinchers. Also *nqimh*.

njiuc - Stem-stitch. *Njiuc-njiuc* is to sew or embroider using the stem-stitch.

njiuv - Scissors.

njiuv-buoz - Scissors hand or handle. A cross-stitch design.

njoux - Saw or the teeth of the saw. A cross-stitch design.

nqimh - Pinchers. Also *njimh*.

nqimh diux - A vine with sharp barbs used for a final dyeing of indigo-dyed cloth to make it black.

nqingh nqou - Tassel, usually short, of silk, cotton, wool, or synthetic yarn or thread.

nqingh nquaiz - Crab.

nqingh nquaiz njimh - Crab pinchers. A grid-stitch design.

nquaav - Chipped or unfinished.

nqun - Chicken's or bird's comb.

nyaanh - Silver.

nyaanh beu - A flat embroidered purse used to carry silver or other valuables that can be rolled up or folded and tucked into the waist sash.

nyaanh biangh - Silver flower. A design done in weave- or grid-stitch which resembles ornamental stick pins cut from sheets of silver which are given as gifts to bride and groom.

nyaanh lengx - Silver coins with holes in the middle such as those used for buttons on a man's vest.

nyietv - To tie up. Also *nyatv*.

nyiuv - Claw or nail.

nyomc - To dye.

nyueic - Tassels, usually long, of silk, cotton, wool, or synthetic material.

nzaangc - Chinese characters. Mien use traditional Chinese characters to record religious ceremonies, geneologies, astrology, folk tales, songs, and poems in books made of hand-made bamboo paper. Although changes have occured over the past hundreds of years, the ritual language is read in a dialect of Cantonese and the literary language, used for poem and songs, is related to some type of Mandarin Chinese. *Nzaangc* now also refers to letters of the alphabet.

paax - A headaddress.

paax-junh - A small triangular embroidered head piece with long ties worn by males when conducting ceremonies.

sa'laqv - Communist.

sa'laqc suix - Thread (white cotton) available from the Vietnamese soldiers.

saa - Spaced, separated, sparce.

saauv suix - Counting threads. Stitches to count the background threads before beginning to embroider.

sen-dauh daai - A long embroidered band worn around the head with the tasseled ends hanging down the back. Worn by men when conducting ceremonies.

setv - End, final, finish.

sieqv - Woman.

sieqv dorn houx - Girl's or woman's pants

sieqv dorn lui - Woman's jacket or coat.

sim - Needle.

sin - Body.

siqc jaauv - Towel or scarf.

siqc jaauv-baeqc - A small white towel often given as a gift.

siqc jaauv-ndaauv - Long towel. White rectangular cloth embroidered on the ends worn across the shoulder by the bride and groom and their attendants during the wedding ceremony. Also called *siqc jaauv-congx* or embroidered towel.

siqv - Red.

som - A barrier or block in a trail usually caused by a fallen tree. A grid-stitch embroidery design.

som maqc - *Som* designs connected together.

som mbaih - *Som* designs in a line or row all joined together.

som saa - *Som* designs separated, not joined together.

som zaqc - Straight *som* design. An old version of the *som* design.

sopc - Pumpkin or squash.

sopc biangh - Pumpkin or squash blossom. An old weave-stitch embroidery design used on the bottom border of women's pants.

sopc bang - Butterfly. An applique design.

sopc bang mbatc - Butterfly antenna. A new cross-stitch design.

48

suangx - Blanket.
suangx-buix - Baby carrier.
suix - Thread.
sux gorc - Rhinocerous.
sux gorc dueiv - Rhinocerous tail. A cross-stitch design.

tiu - To pick something up with a hook.
tongv - Bucket, barrel.

waanh - To hang down, dangle.
wuom - Water.
wuom-gaeng - Water insect, water bug. An old weave-stitch design.
Wuonh Guangv congx - One of the older weave-stitch designs used on the bottom border of women's pants. *Wuonh Guangv* is a person's name or just the name of this design. Sometimes called *m'guangv congx*.

yangh - Yellow.
yienx - A small carved wooden printing stamp used on certain kinds of spirit money burned during religious ceremonies.

zaqc - Straight.
zangx - Steamer.
zangx-piaeng - The bottom of a steamer made of woven bamboo. A cross-stitch design.
zaux - Foot or leg.
ziem - A decorative edging stitch which looks like a diagonal running stitch on the back side of the fabric, a chain stitch on the front. Executed by looping the thread for the new stitch through the "legs" of the previous stitch and taking a diagonal stitch in the background fabric. Used on turbans and sashes.
zorx yoc - A kneeling cloth or blanket used by bride and groom during the kneeling ceremony. It is also used as a saddle blanket on the horse transporting the bride's father to the wedding ceremony.
zou - Bead.
zou-baaih - A fringe of tassels that hangs down from the bride's wedding hat covering her face.
zou-nzenc - Tubular wound glass Chinese beads used on old ornaments.
zoux ndaangh - An important merit-making ceremony.

A variation of the top border on a pair of woman's pants.

GLOSSARY OF LAO MIEN EMBROIDERY DESIGNS

STEM STITCH, *NJIUC*

Njiuc, or stem-stitch-worked over one thread vertically, and horizontally, it goes over 4 threads, back under 2 threads, over 4 threads, etc. forming a solid line of slightly diagonal stitches. Three rows are almost always placed together to underline or separate rows or sections of designs.

njiuc - ßtem stitch, done in three rows with *congx-sieqv* and *som* designs.

WEAVE-STITCH, *CONGX-JIEMC*

The following four rows of weave-stitch designs are used on the bottom section of women's pants' panels. Each row represents a set that is usually used together. The first one in each row is the one used on the very bottom of the section and is called *congx-dorn*, small embroidery, since it is usually narrower than the middle one which is called big embroidery, *domh congx*. The last one in each row is called edging or finishing embroidery, *congx-setv*, and is at the top of the section.

congx-dorn   *domh congx*   *congx-setv*

congx-mbiaapc- ceremonial fan
congx-ceix - Sharp spike made from bamboo. Made to trap big animals or as protection from people around rice fields.
congx-nzaangc- Chinese characters

congx-dorn *domh congx* *congx-setv*

Wuonh Guangv congx- Wuonh Guangv embroidery

congx-dorn *domh congx* *congx-setv*

sopc biangh- squash flower

congx-dorn *domh congx* *congx-setv*

Weave design similar to *sopc biangh* seen on an old white sash and on old pants from Luang Prabang area.

ADDITIONAL WEAVE-STITCH DESIGNS

domh jienv-jiemc,
jienv-ngau
big weave-stitch gibbon,
crooked gibbon

domh jienv,
buoz-zaux camv
big gibbon
lots of hands and feet

jienv dorn
little gibbon

jienv-saa
loosely spaced gibbon

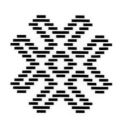

congx-nzaangc
Chinese characters

congx-sieqv
little girl embroidery

ga'nyorc dorn
cinq-jiouc dueiv
small spider
cing-jiouc bird's tail

ga'nyorc
mba'hinx dueiv
spider
mba'hinx bird's tail

domh ga'nyorc
big spider

ga'nyorc-benx
enriched spider design

dungz-dorn deih
baby pig's hoof

(ga')maeqc mbeux
popcorn
gaam-zaiv-neix
orange stem

ga'nyorc-nquaav
unfinished, chipped spider

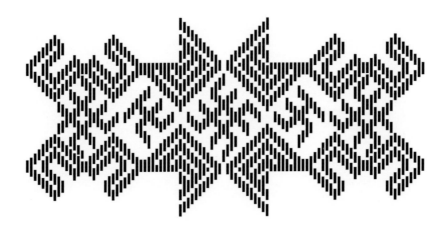

ga'nyorc-jieqv

black spider- In this grouping the chipped design or the baby pig's hoofs are often done in black.

wuom-gaeng
water bug

wuom-gaeng
water bug

wuom-gaeng
water bug

mba'ong-don
thunder stool

da'jungh ndiangx
da'jungh tree

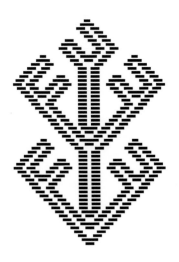

da'jungh ndiangx
da'jungh tree

da'jungh ndiangx
da'jungh tree

nyaanh biangh
silver flower

nyaanh biangh
silver flower

nyaanh biangh
silver flower

nyaanh biangh-
silver flower

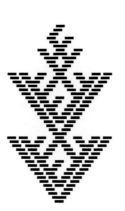

old design, no name

mbiauz-mbungv
fish bone

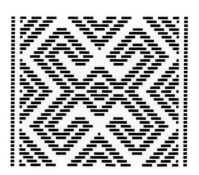

old design, no name

GRID-STITCH, *CONGX-TIU*

domh ga'nyorc
big spider

ga'nyorc dorn
little spider

jienv-tiu
grid-stitch gibbon

congx-niouv
twisted design

som

som zaqc
straight *som*

som dorn
little *som*

som maqc, som mbaih
joined *som, som* in a line

som saa
sparce or spaced *som*

lomh zeuv
lomh zeuv design

lomh zeuv dorn
little *lomh zeuv* design

lomh zeuv ngau
crooked *lomh zeuv* design

lomh zeuv nyiuv
lomh zeuv claws

ga'nyorh nquaav
chipped, unfinished spider

nqingh nquaiz njimh
crab claws

nqingh nquaiz njimh and *fam*
crab claws and filler

ga'nyorc-joih

Bunch of spiders - Term given to groupings of various *ga'nyorc, som,* and *lomh zeuv* designs done either in grid- or weave-stitch.

58

nyaanh biangh dorn
small silver flower

congx-caengx
support design, refering to the crossing support rows

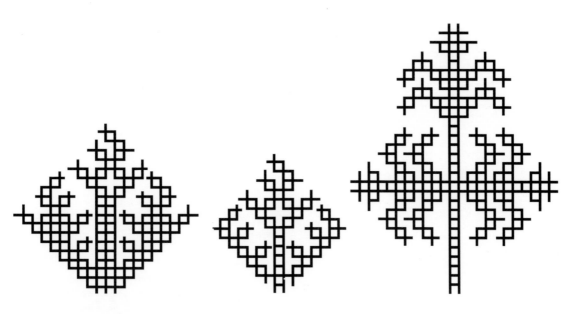

congx-caengx
support design, Thai style
with double central row

congx-caengx
support design, Lao style
with single central row

no name

CROSS-STITCH, *CONGX-NYIETV*

njoux
saw, sawtooth

The Thai and Sayabouri Mien tend to use more rows of cross-stitch for this design than do the northern Lao Mien.

This design is usually bordered by 3 rows of *njiuc*; on only one side by the northern Lao Mien, and on both top and bottom by the Thai and Sayabouri Mien.

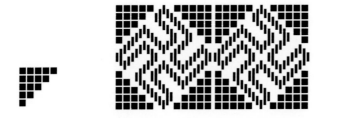 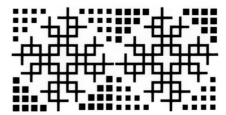

nyietv-hlaengx

cross-stitch sections. Triangular sections used as fillers in spaces between weave- and grid-stitch designs.

m'zuv huaa
Chinese for a kind of flower

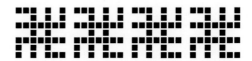

buoz-zaux camv
many hands and feet

Janx-gekv tei, Janx-taiv biauv
Chinese stairs, Thai houses

Janx-gekv tei, Janx-taiv biauv
Chinese stairs, Thai houses

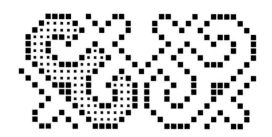

nda'maauh nyiuv, nda'maauh ndopv
tiger claw, tiger skin

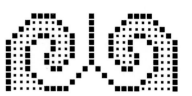

nda'maauh nyiuv
tiger claws

domh nda'maauh nyiuv
big tiger claws

domh ngau
big hook

ngau dorn
little hook

njiuv-buoz
scissors handle

no name

no name except *congx* S

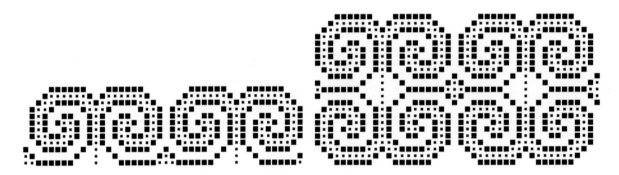

baeqc miuh biangh
Hmong flower

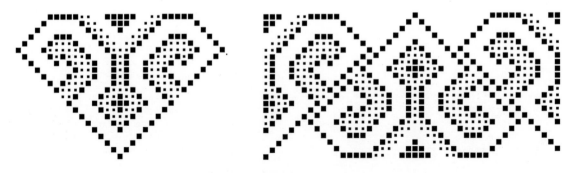

nda'maauh biorngh, nda'maauh m'normh
tiger forehead, tiger ears

domh biangh dueiv
big blossom tails

domh biangh benx
embellished big blossoms

jung-hungh, jung-hinc
dragon, rainbow

jung hungh, janx-dorn ngamv
dragon, rainbow with little people squatting

congx-gapv, guaax dang don
box, puzzle embroidery, *guaax dang* stool

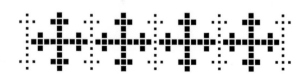

congx-gapv, jouv coix biangh
box or puzzle, Chinese leek flower

jouv coix biangh
Chinese leek flower

GLOSSARY OF LAO MIEN EMBROIDERY DESIGNS

buih dorh
weight on a balance scale

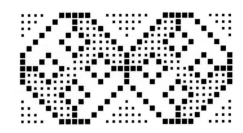

mba'hnoi-biangh
sunflower

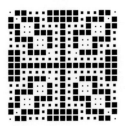

zangx-piaeng
rice steamer

no name

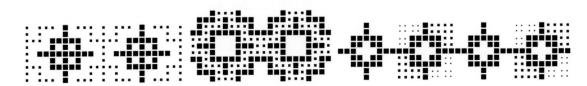

Luh Guon louc
row, vine of *Luh Guon*

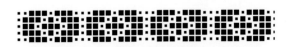
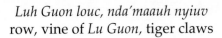

Luh Guon louc, nda'maauh nyiuv
row, vine of *Lu Guon*, tiger claws

Luh Guon-yienx
Luh Guon-fim
Luh Guon's stamp

Fim is the inside part of certain plants like onions, bananas, ginger.

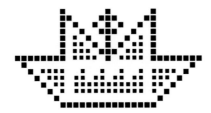

Faam-Cing nqun-
comb of the *Faam-Cing* bird

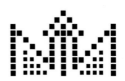

Faam-Cing dueiv-
tail of the *Faam-Cing* bird

COMPOSITE CROSS-STITCH DESIGNS

Faam-Cing nqun
comb of the *Faam-Cing* bird

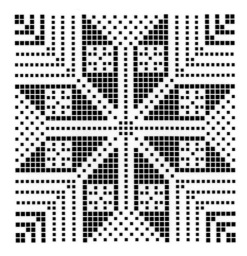

sux gorc dueiv, baeqc miuh caengx
rhinocerous tail, Hmong umbrella

zangx-piaeng
rice steamer

zangx-piaeng
rice steamer

buih dorh benx
embellished *bui dorh* design

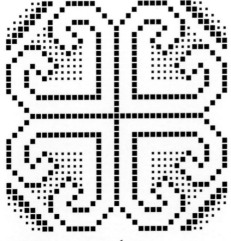

congx-benx
embellished design (copied from the Hmong)

nda'maauh m'normz gapv
tiger ears put together

nda'maauh dopv
tiger skin

congx-benx
embellished embroider

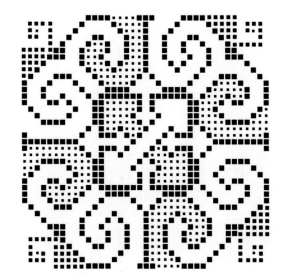

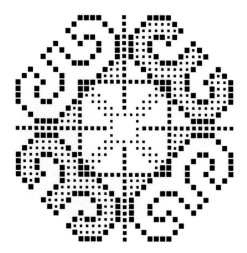

congx-benx, congx-gapv
embellished or combined designs

congx-benx, congx-gapv
embellished or combined designs

Janx-gekv tei, Janx-taiv biauv
Chinese stairs, Thai houses

jung hungh
dragon, rainbow

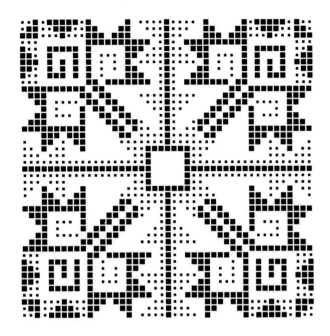

domh biangh
big blossoms

Designs from an old embroidered wedding square.

Designs from an old embroidered wedding square.

BIBLIOGRAPHY

Adams, Monni. 1974. "Dress and Design in Highland Southeast Asia: The Hmong (Miao) and the Yao" in *Textile Museum Journal* 4:51–67.

Beard, Tim, Betsey Warrick, and Kao Cho Saefong, eds. 1993. *Loz-Hnoi, Loz- Hnoi Uov, In the Old, Old Days. Traditional Stories of the Iu- Mienh.* Vol. 1, Berkeley: Laotian Handcraft Center.

Butler-Diaz, Jacqueline. 1970. *Yao Design.* Bangkok: The Siam Society.

Campbell, Margaret. 1978. *From the Hands of the Hills.* Hong Kong: Media Transasia Ltd.

Cooke, David. 1990. *Iu Mienh Dictionary,* Turloch, CA.

Court, Chris. 1991. *"Mien"* in Thai Hill Tribes Phrasebook, by David Bradley. Berkeley, CA: Lonely Planet Publications, Inc.

Crystal, Eric and Kaota Saepharn. 1992. "Iu-Mien: Highland Southeast Asian Community and Culture in a California Context" in *Minority Cultures of Laos: Kammu, Lua', Lahu, Hmong and Mien*, Judy Lewis, ed. Rancho Cordova, CA: Southeast Asia Community Resource Center, Folsom-Cordova Unified School District.

Hanks, Jane Richardson. 1965. "A Yao Wedding," in *Ethnographic Notes on Northern Thailand.* Ithaca: Cornell University, Department of Asian Studies Southeast Asia Program, Data Pater NO. 58. 47–66.

Hoffman, Elizabeth. 1982. *Dress and Acculturation: Clothing Transitions of the Mien.* Masters Thesis, Oregon State University.

Kandre, Peter. 1967. "Autonomy and Integration of Social Systems: The Mien ('Yao" or "Man") Mountain Population and Their Neighbors" in *Southeast Asian Tribes, Minorities, and Nations*, Peter E. Kunstadter, ed. Princeton, New Jersey: Princeton University Press.

Kandre, Peter K. and Lej Tsan Kuej. 1965. "Aspects of Wealth-Accumulation, Ancestor Worship and Household Stability Among the Mien-Yao" in *Felicitation Volumes of Southeast-Asian Studies*, Vol. 1, 129–148. Bangkok: The Siam Society.

Kitagawa, Akiko. 1992. *Yao Stitchery,* Kyoto: Shikosha Publishing Co. Ltd.

Lemoine, Jacques. 1982. *Yao Ceremonial Paintings.* Bangkok: White Lotus Co. Ltd.

—— 1983, "Yao Religion and Society" in *Highlanders of Thailand*, John McKinnon and Wanat Bhruksasre, eds., 195–211. Kuala Lumpur: Oxford University Press.

Lewis, Paul and Elaine Lewis. 1984. *Peoples of the Golden Triangle: Six Tribes in Thailand.* London: Thames & Hudson, Ltd.

Moore-Howard, Patricia. 1990. *The Iu Mien.* Sacramento: Sacramento City Unified School District.

Sharp, Ruth B. 1965. "It's Expensive To Be a Yao" in *Ethnographic Notes on Northern Thailand*, 36–39. L.M. Hanks, J.R. Hanks, and Lauriston Sharp, eds. Data Paper No. 58, Southeast Asia Program. Ithaca, New York: Cornell University.

Thongkum, Theraphan L. 1991. *Passport for Traveling in the Hills.* Bangkok: Linguistics Research Unit, Faculty of Arts, Chulalongkorn University. Thai and English.

PHOTO CREDITS:

Ann Goldman (AG): 1–3, 5–7, 10, 11, 13, 14, 17–19, 21–26, 28, 29, 31, 32, 34–37, 39–41, 47, 49, 56, 58, 60, 61, 63, 68–75, 78–81, 83, 85, 86, 89, 91, 95, 100, 101, 103, 105, 108–112.

Sandra Cate (SC): 4, 8, 9, 20, 30, 38, 42–46, 51–53, 57, 59, 62, 64–67, 77, 82, 90, 92–94, 97, 106, 107.

Linda D'Ari (LD): 15, 16, 54, 55, 84, 96, 98, 99, 102.

Sylvia Lombard (SL): 12, 27, 33, 48, 50, 76, 87, 88.

Mey Meng Saeteun: 104.

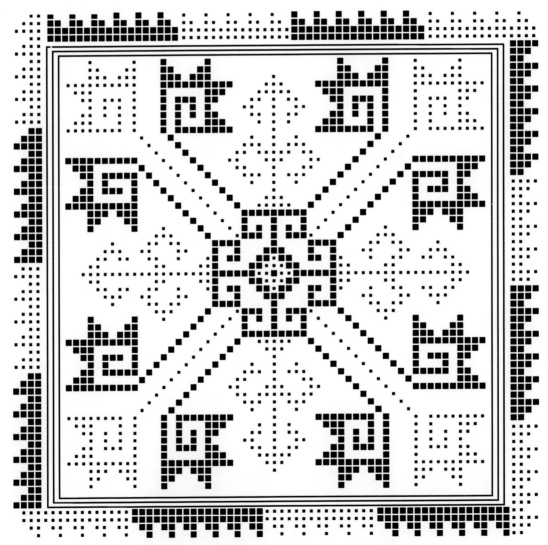

A variation of *domh biangh* or big blossom.